JOHN ROSEMOND'S SIX-POINT PLAN FOR RAISING HAPPY, HEALTHY CHILDREN

JOHN ROSEMOND'S SIX-POINT PLAN FOR RAISING HAPPY, HEALTHY CHILDREN

JOHN K. ROSEMOND

ANDREWS AND McMEEL
A UNIVERSAL PRESS SYNDICATE COMPANY
KANSAS CITY

Designed and illustrated by Barrie Maguire

Library of Congress Cataloging in Publication Data

Rosemond, John K., 1947–
    Six-point plan for raising happy, healthy children / John K. Rosemond.
    p. cm.
    ISBN 0-8362-2806-5 : $8.95
    1. Child rearing—United States. 2. Parenting—United States. 3. Child
rearing—United States—Miscellanea. 4. Parenting—United States—
Miscellanea. I. Title.
HQ769.R714 1989   89-30316
649'.1—dc19   CIP

First Printing, March 1989
Twentieth Printing, April 1997

For Eric and Amy

CONTENTS

ACKNOWLEDGMENTS

I want to express my appreciation to . . .

All the good folks at both the *Charlotte Observer* and *Better Homes and Gardens* magazine, for giving me so much support and encouragement over the years.

All my clients, for trusting me enough to let me come into your lives and learn something.

The Knight-Ridder Wire and all of the newspapers across the United States and Canada that carry my column, for giving me an audience.

Everyone who's ever come to hear me speak, for laughing at all the right moments.

Willie, the *real* expert, for your love and patient support.

READ
THIS
FIRST!

O nce upon a time, people got married, had children, and reared them. It wasn't something they spent a lot of time fussing and fretting over. It was just something they did, along with planting seeds in the spring and harvesting them in the fall. If they came up against a childrearing problem, they sought advice from grandparents and great-aunts and older brothers and sisters who'd already started their families. These were the experts of not-so-long ago, and they gave practical advice based on real-life experiences.

Along came a war and then a baby boom. Young parents took their children and went looking for the promised land. From the ashes of the extended family rose an entirely different class of childrearing experts, ones with degrees and nameplates on their doors, and large, mahogany desks.

It wasn't long before rhetoric replaced reality as the primary shaper of our childrearing practices. Nonsense replaced common sense. American families became child-centered, and American parents became permissive and democratic. Not surprisingly, American children became self-centered, self-indulgent, spoiled, sassy, and out of control.

Over the last forty years or so, we've taken the very practical and commonsensical job of raising children, dressed it in fancy language, and turned it into something very abstract and, therefore, difficult. What the "experts" haven't romanticized, sentimentalized, and idealized, they've scrutinized and analyzed to such an extent that we are no longer able to see the forest for all the obsessing we do over the trees.

In the process, childrearing—or *parenting,* as it's now called—has been transformed into a pseudo-intellectual "science," something people think they must strain their brains at in order to do properly. But parenting is anything but an intellectual endeavor. In fact, the more you strain your brain at it, the more likely you are to find yourself lost among the trees.

Good parenting does not emanate primarily from the head; it comes from the heart and the gut. It is not a matter of long, hard thought, but a matter of how intuitively sensitive you are to *your* needs and the needs of your child, and a matter of how firmly grounded you are in the soil of common sense. Parents who think too much tend to say things like, "Raising a child is the hardest thing I've ever done." I understand. I used to feel that way myself. Then I stopped thinking so much about it, stopped obsessing over all the little details, stopped worrying about whether one wrong decision was going to ruin my children for life, and started paying at least as much attention to my own needs and the needs of my marriage as I did to my kids. That's when raising children became relatively easy and enjoyable.

Because I write a syndicated newspaper column as well as books and magazine articles on the subject, people think I'm an expert at raising children. Well, they're right! I *am* an expert at raising children. Their names are Eric and Amy. At the time of this writing, Eric is coming up on his twentieth birthday and is well into his second year at North Carolina State University. He's in an engineering program, but wants to become a pilot. Amy is sixteen and close to finishing her third year of high school. She isn't sure what she wants to do next, and I don't blame her. Time is *not* of the essence in her young life. I couldn't ask for better kids. They're smart, funny, creative, and determined.

I've become an expert at raising them through trial-and-error, which is the only way anyone ever becomes an expert parent. I'm not an expert by virtue of having obtained a graduate degree in child psychology. In fact, my formal schooling did more to hinder my ability to raise children than help it. Graduate school filled my head with a lot of abstractions and theory about children and childrearing, but did nothing toward advancing my common sense. It caused me to think a lot about the "right" way to raise a child, but the harder I thought, the more I lost touch with my intuitions.

Raising children is not fundamentally difficult, but the "experts" made it sound difficult, and we made the mistake of believing them. After all, they had fancy degrees, didn't they? In fact, their rhetoric often concealed more than it revealed. If you strip away all that fancy, intellectual language, however, you'll discover some basic, timeless truths that serve to make childrearing quite simple. The problem with these truths is that they are neither romantic nor sentimental. They are realistic, pragmatic, and hard-headed. For example: The Ultimate Purpose of Parenting is to help our children out of our lives.

I'm writing this book in order to share my understanding of that, and other, equally unsentimental truths. I write from the point-of-view of someone who's been a husband for nearly twenty-one years and a father for nearly twenty. Those are the primary sources of my expertness. Being a psychologist has helped me gain access to the media, but it's helped relatively little in gaining access to the truth about raising children.

I happen to think it's high time we returned to a more traditional, commonsensical vision of childrearing. That's what this book is all about. It's about putting the marriage first, expecting children to obey, expecting and enabling them to contribute meaningfully to the family, and giving them everything they need along with a conservative amount of what they simply want. It's about trimming the fat off the roast. None of the concepts presented in this book are new. They stood the test of time for countless generations. We only misplaced them when we tried to make a "science and technology" out of raising children in order to keep it in step with "progress."

During our first few years of parenthood, my wife Willie and I read all the right books and did all the supposedly right things those supposed experts advised, but everything went wrong anyway. They said to respect Eric as an equal, but the more respect we showed him, the less he showed us. They said families should be democratic, but the more democratic we were, the more of a tyrant Eric became. They said it was wrong to control children, but the less control we exercised, the more out-of-control he was. The more wrong things went, the more guilty we felt, the more insecure Eric was, and the more crazy we all were.

In time, we discovered that the more childrearing books we read, the more we believed that experts had the answers, and the more we lost touch with and trust in ourselves. And so, about three years into the game, we stopped listening to the experts and began raising Eric not by the book, but by the heart and the gut. In that fourth year of Eric's life and first year of Amy's, Willie and I took our first steps toward becoming experts at raising children.

My one purpose in writing this book is to put you, the reader, in touch with your capacity to be an expert at raising your children. I want to put you back in touch with common sense. I want you to understand that while raising children is not always fun, it does not have to be difficult, and it can always be rewarding. In short, I want to help you learn to depend on yourself in raising your children.

After all, you're an expert, too. You may not know it, but you are—just like me.

Enjoy!

JOHN ROSEMOND
P.O. Box 4124
Gastonia, N.C. 28054

POINT
ONE

The Parent-Centered Family

Because I'm regarded as an expert on parenting, people are forever asking me questions about raising children. These questions vary tremendously. In fact, I can honestly say that no two people have ever asked the same exact question. On the other hand, despite that variety, all parents really seem to be asking this one fundamental question: "John, what's the *secret*, the *key* to raising a happy, healthy child?"

The question sounds like it requires a long and rather complex answer. Within recent years, in fact, quite a number of books have been written in exactly that attempt, and we certainly haven't seen the last of them. But after twenty-one years of being a husband and twenty years of being a father, I've come to the conclusion that "The Answer" is not that complicated after all.

Actually, there are *two* equally simple ways of answering the question. The choice depends on whether I'm talking to a parent or parents who are married, or a parent who is single. I'm going to take first things first and reserve my discussion of single parenting until later. In any case, most of what I have to say about being married and raising children has its parallel in single parenthood.

For those of you who are married, the secret to raising happy, healthy children is to give more attention to the marriage than you give to the children. If you succeed at that, your children will turn out just fine.

That answer often surprises people because it isn't what they're expecting. They're set up to hear me say something about building a child's self-esteem by giving praise or quality time or something equally child-centered. Instead, my answer has more to do with the health of the family as a *unit* than with any particular person in the family. What I'm saying is that by ordering priorities properly within your family, you give your children the greatest guarantee of happiness you can possibly ever give.

"My Children Come First!"

A number of years ago, I conducted a series of parenting workshops for working mothers. I began each session by walking into the room and writing "In my family, my children come first" on the blackboard. Turning around, I would then ask for a show of hands from those women who subscribed to that particular statement of principle. Hands would shoot up everywhere, and many of the women would turn to one another and smile and nod as if to say, "Why, of course! We all realize the necessity of that, now don't we?" To me, however, those hands and those unspoken exchanges of consensus reflected the degree to which we, as a culture, have misplaced family priorities.

In the years since World War II, we have become increasingly, and neurotically, obsessed with the raising of children. Something that used to be a fairly commonsensical responsibility has taken on the trappings of science. Along the way, child-rearing has become "parenting" with all of its high-pressure implications. In the process, we have elevated children to a position of prominence within families that they do not warrant, have certainly not earned, and definitely do not benefit from. Within the child-centered family, the implicit understanding is that the children are the most important people in

the family, and the parent-child relationship is the most important relationship. And the more child-centered the American
family has become, the more demandingly self-centered American children have become. And the more demanding children
have become, the more demanding the task of raising them has
become.

In order to justify the frustrations inherent to this upside-
down state of affairs, we've invented the idea that raising children is necessarily difficult. Time and again, I hear parents
complain that it's the hardest thing they've ever done. But
underneath the complaint I sense a feeling of pride, as if they
need raising children to be difficult in order to feel like they're
doing a good job.

Well, if you want raising children to be difficult, you need
only put them first in your family, and it will be. By putting
your children first in your family, you guarantee they will
become manipulative, demanding, and unappreciative of anything and everything you do for them. You guarantee they will
grow up believing they can do as they please, that it's unfair of
you to expect them to lift a finger of responsibility around the
home, and that it's your bounden duty to give them everything
they want and serve them in every conceivable way. Putting
children first in the family further guarantees that you will
experience parenthood as one of the most frustrating and unre-
warding things you've ever done. It further guarantees the
ultimate unhappiness of your children, because happiness is
achieved *only* by accepting responsibility for one's self, not by
being led to believe that someone else is responsible for you.

Again, it's a question of priorities. In a two-parent family,
the marriage *must* come first. After all, the marriage created the
family, and the marriage sustains it. The marriage *preceded* the
children, and is meant to *succeed* them. If you *don't* put your
marriage first, and keep it there, it's likely to become a mirage.

The Life of a Cell

I describe the marriage-centered/parent-centered family in
much the same way a biologist describes a cell. The biologist

defines a cell as the basic building block of biological life. At the functional center of any particular cell, there is a nucleus which "runs the show," so to speak. It is the executive authority within that cell. As such, it regulates the cell's metabolism, reproduction, and other essential functions. It also mediates that cell's relationship to its neighbor-cells, and determines what role the cell is going to perform within the larger organism of which it is a part. Furthermore, the biologist knows that if the nucleus of the cell is healthy and performing its role properly, the cell itself will be healthy and capable of making a positive contribution to its host organism. On the other hand, if the nucleus is not healthy, if it has been disturbed by disease or the invasion of foreign matter, it becomes less capable of performing its role, and the cell begins to deteriorate.

In a similar way, the family is the basic unit of social life. It is a social cell within a larger social organism called society. A family has a nucleus, too. In a two-parent family, the nucleus is the marriage. In a single-parent family, the nucleus is the single parent. Likewise, if the needs of the marriage or single parent are being met, then the family as a system will be healthy, and each individual within it will be healthy as well. In other words, if the marriage is being taken care of, or if the single parent is taking care of her/himself, the children will, in all likelihood, be fine. They will feel protected. They will feel secure. They will have a clear sense of identity, and they will therefore have a foundation upon which to build good self-esteem.

This means that in a two-parent family, the marriage must be held in the highest regard. It must be the most important relationship within the family, and it must be more important than *any single individual* within the family. All too often, however, people give lip service to that idea, but then turn around and *behave* as if the parent-child relationship is the most significant relationship within the family. At the heart of that inconsistency lies the most destructive myth ever manufactured and sold to parents. It is the completely untrue, but almost universally subscribed to idea, that children *need* a lot of attention.

Myth? That's right, as in make-believe, not true. At best, it's a misunderstanding, born of misguided idealism. At worst, and especially when it's handed down from on high from a so-called parenting expert, it's a lie. In the last forty years or so, the "Children-Need-Lots-of-Attention" myth has exerted tremendous influence upon our childrearing practices with absolutely disastrous results for children, their parents, and families as a whole.

Attention: The First Addiction

Children do *not* require a lot of attention. Children need very little attention, in fact. Let me help you digest this hard-to-swallow tidbit of news by talking, for a moment, about children and food.

Children need food. But they don't need a lot of it. If you persist in giving a child more food than he or she needs, that child will become dependent upon continuing to receive excessive amounts of food. If you continue to feed that dependency, it will grow into an obsession that will function as a powerful, driving force in that child's life. The child's sense of well-being will lean increasingly on the idea that in order to feel secure, he must have ready access to food. Eventually, the child will become a food addict, and that addiction will hang like a stone around the child's neck, encumbering the growth of self-esteem.

Now go back and reread the previous paragraph, substituting the word "attention" wherever you see the word "food." Go ahead, I'll wait.

Done? Quite revealing, isn't it? You see, it is as absurd to say that children need a lot of attention as it is to say that children need a lot of food. Too much attention is every bit as damaging as too much food. No one would argue that it is part of our job as parents to set limits on how much food a child may consume. It follows, therefore, that it's also part of our job to set limits on how much attention a child is allowed to consume within a family. But many, if not most, parents fail to set adequate limits on the amount of attention their children can expect to receive. So in many, if not most families, you find a child or children who can't seem to get enough attention.

You probably know one: A child who constantly interrupts adult conversations, wants "in on the action" when his or her parents are being affectionate toward one another, talks incessantly (and loudly), acts silly, as if all of life is a performance, and given the choice, would rather be inside with a group of adults than outside playing with a group of children.

We're talking about an addict. And the child who develops an addiction to attention stands a better-than-average likelihood of some day transferring that dependency to drugs, alcohol, or self-destructive, high-risk behavior of some other form. At the very least, the attention-addicted child may never really grow up, may never truly attain emotional emancipation.

Earlier, I compared a family to a cell. A family is also structured somewhat like a solar system, which is, come to think of it, a galactic cell. At the center of a solar system, there is source of energy which nurtures and stabilizes the system. Around this central core revolve a number of planets in various stages of "maturity."

Likewise, a family needs a powerful, stabilizing, and nurturing source of energy at its center. The only people who are qualified to sit in that position of power and responsibility are parents. Their job is to define, organize, lead, nurture, and sustain the family.

Children are the "planets" in this system. When they are very young, they orbit close to the parent-sun because they need lots of nurturing and guidance. As they grow, their orbits increase steadily in circumference so that by their late teens or early twenties, they should be capable of escaping the pull of their parents' gravity and embarking upon lives of their own. Our children's ultimate task is to move away from us, and our task is to help them. Allowing a child to bask in the spotlight of attention, however, encumbers the child's ability to establish greater and greater degrees of independence. A child cannot be the center of attention in a family and move away from that center at the same time. It's either one or the other.

If you put a child in the family spotlight, you create the illusion that he or she is the most important person in the family. That center-stage position is too cozy, too warm, too comfortable, and the child who sits there will want to stay there—basking in the warm glow as long as he or she can.

In 1972, a group of researchers selected a sample of high school graduates from around the country. Four years later, they polled these graduates and found that approximately 25 percent were still living with their parents. In 1984, these same researchers polled a similar sample from the high school graduating class of 1980. This time, they found that nearly 50 percent were still single and living with their parents. Those statistics tell us that today's children are having increasingly serious difficulty emancipating themselves. Either we are clinging to them, or they are clinging to us, or both.

Growing Up

For most of the first seven years of my life, my mother was a single parent. During this time, she and I lived with my grandmother in a small apartment in what is now the historic district of Charleston, South Carolina. In those days, it was just the "old part of town."

During the day, Grandma worked and Mom attended classes at the College of Charleston, working toward her degree in biology. At night and on weekends, she worked part-time at the post office, sorting mail. For several years, I was cared for in our home by a woman named Gertie Mae. The year before I started school, I attended a preschool program. My mother was a busy person in those days. She had to be, what with college, a job, and a child. There were many nights when she wasn't at home to tuck me in, which Grandma did in her stead, always reading to me from classics such as *Wind in the Willows* and Kipling's *Just-So Stories*.

When Mom *was* home, she was often studying. She didn't spend much time with me as a child because she didn't have much time to spend. In fact, she discouraged me from even hanging around her much. When I did, she would look at me sternly and say something like, "You're underfoot. You do not need to be hanging around me now. You should be outside, finding something to do." With that, she would usher me outdoors where I'd find myself sharing the sidewalk with other children who'd also been kicked out of their houses. But we would be happy together, just being kids. Even though Mom had relatively little time for me and expected me to be fairly independent, I never felt unloved or rejected or uncared for. Quite the contrary. I felt *very* loved and *very* independent at the same time. Mom was always there when I needed her, but she was also quick to tell me when my need was not *need* at all, but simply unnecessary *want*.

In retrospect, I now realize that shooing me out from "underfoot" was simply Mom's way of letting me know she had a life of her own, separate from being my mother, and that I had a life of *my* own, as well. By not allowing me to become overly dependent upon her presence and attention, Mom gave me permission to grow up and away from her.

That's exactly what the job of parent is all about. It's about helping our children get out of our lives. When I say that to an audience, some people laugh and some look shocked, as if I've just said something sacrilegious or obscene or both. But it's no joke, and I don't say it for shock value. It's the truth. When you strip away all the intellectual rhetoric and the flowery sentiment, you realize that the purpose of raising children is simply to help them out of our lives and into successful lives of their own. It's called emancipation. But emancipation is not an event that takes place at age twenty or thereabouts. It's a *process* that takes twenty or so years to unfold and come to fruition. And it's not that complicated, or even that difficult. It simply means doing for your child what my mother did for me.

Out of practical necessity, Mom became an expert at defining for me the difference between my needs and my wants. If I truly needed her, she was always there. On the other hand, if I wanted her to do something for me that I could do for myself or do without, she was quick to instruct me accordingly. I was not the center of attention in her life, and she made sure that as I grew, she became less and less the center of attention in mine. I had growing up to do, and she pointed the way.

Making that distinction is the most *essential* of a parent's responsibilities. At first, the parent makes it for the child. Eventually, the child becomes capable of making it for himself. That's called "growing up," and that's what being a child is all about. It's *not* about getting lots of attention.

This is why it's so important that parents realize that the amount of attention given a child very quickly reaches the point of diminishing returns. Once that point is reached, that attention is more detrimental than beneficial to the emancipation process. As that process unfolds, so does a child's capacity for initiative, resourcefulness, creativity, self-sufficiency, achievement, and therefore, self-esteem. So when I tell parents to pay more attention to their marriages than they do their children, I'm not advocating selfish neglect. You pay more attention to the marriage for the child's sake as well as your own.

The Games People Play

For the marriage to be Number One in a family means, among other things, that the man and woman function primarily in the roles of husband and wife. Those are, after all, the roles they committed themselves to on the day they were married. All too often, however, when a couple begins having children, the roles of husband and wife begin receding into the background. Slowly but surely, the female stops functioning primarily in the role of wife and, instead, begins functioning primarily in the role of mother. Simultaneously, the male shifts from his role as husband into the role of primary breadwinner. This process happens unconsciously. It's as if the birth of a child activates cultural programs that say, "Wife, your primary obligation is now to your children," and "Husband, your primary obligation is now to ensure permanent financial security for your family." And with that, the original contract—the commitment to one another as husband and wife—begins breaking down. As this insidious shift in roles takes place, the wife (now mother) begins to measure her self-esteem against how well-behaved her children are and how well they perform academically, socially, and in the various activities to which she feels obligated to chauffeur them. Likewise, the husband (now breadwinner) begins to measure his self-esteem against how much money he makes, how quickly he climbs the career ladder, and how much social prestige he secures for himself and his family.

Unbeknownst to them, these two people are now moving in opposite, noncomplementary directions. The wife becomes increasingly involved with her children, increasingly obsessed with and consumed by the concerns and responsibilities of parenthood. Likewise, the husband becomes increasingly immersed in his career. He begins spending more and more time at the office. When he comes home, he often brings the office with him—if not physically, in the form of a bulging briefcase, then mentally, in the form of headaches, worries, and other forms of stress. If his wife wants a relationship with him, she finds she has to maneuver around his preoccupation with work. On the other hand, if the husband comes home looking for a relationship with his wife, he discovers that in order to have one, he must maneuver around her preoccupations with raising children.

As this divergence takes place, resentment begins to build in the relationship. The husband begins to feel increasingly angry over the fact that his wife gives more time to the children than she does to him, even when he is at home. The wife becomes increasingly angry at the fact that her husband gives more time to his career than he does to her. The wife sees her half of the picture; the husband, his. But neither is able to see the whole, and with it, their own part in the process. Instead, each defines the situation in terms of the other person's "fault."

Now, in our culture, we don't do a very good job of preparing people for relationship problems of this sort. So instead of putting their cards on the table, these two people begin playing games to express and deal with their pent-up resentments. The games they play with one another are always variations on the theme of "Guess What's on My Mind."

One of the most typical "Guess What's on My Mind" games these two people are likely to play is a game you may recognize. It's a game called "Who Had the Worst Day?" If you don't recognize it, or you need your memory refreshed, here's a description of this peculiar sport.

"Who Had the Worst Day?" begins around 5:30 in the afternoon, when Dad arrives home from work. I'm going to describe the game in terms of the way it might be played in a more or less "traditional" American family—one in which Dad

14

works at making a living, and Mom works at raising the children—but this same game can be played even if both people have jobs outside the family.

To continue, Dad pulls into the driveway and the news travels throughout the house: "Dad's home!" Immediately, the children begin bouncing around wildly, so as to greet Dad properly when he walks through the door. Dad parks the car, gets out, and immediately assumes his slumped and crumpled "I've Had a Bad Day" position.

Dad the Downtrodden shuffles up to the house, dragging his briefcase behind him. As he opens the door, he's met by a stampede of children—each of them wanting his attention.

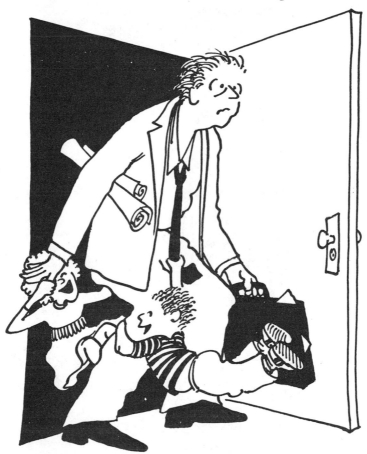

Each wants to tell Dad what he/she did that day. They want to tell on each other. They're yelling things at him, like, "Did you bring me anything?" and "Take us to the store, please, Daddy, please, will you Daddy, please, huh?"

Let's not forget Mom! She's standing in the background, viewing this chaos from the shadows. Her version of the "I've Had a Bad Day" position, however, is quite different from her husband's.

Mom's pupils are dilated, her nostrils are flared, and every vein in her neck is taut. She doesn't have to say anything,

because every nuance of her body language screams, *"I've had it!"* If she says anything at all, it's something along the lines of, "Well, it's about time you got home from your eight-hour vacation, Big Guy. Now, it's time for *you* to find out what it's like to be a parent. From this moment on, they're all yours!"

And the game is on! Occasionally, the husband "wins." He persuades his wife to sympathize with what a bad day he's had, how rotten his boss is, how hard he works, blah, blah, blah, and his wife cooperates by allowing him to collapse in his favorite easy chair and zonk out behind the paper or in front of the television, while she keeps the kids occupied in another room.

Sometimes the wife "wins." Her hang-dog husband takes the kids out for a ride to let her relax, and he picks up supper at a Chinese restaurant so she doesn't have to cook, and he might even—if Mom's *real* lucky—put the kids to bed that night.

In the final analysis, however, "Who Had the Worst Day?" is a game with no winners. It's a game people play because they've already *lost* something, and that something is a proper sense of their priorities. Somewhere, back down the line, they misplaced the fact that the marriage is the most important commitment in their lives. Until they rediscover it, they will continue to become increasingly isolated in roles that do not complement one another and increasingly distant in terms of communication and intimacy.

It should come as no surprise to hear that the divorce rate among people forty-five and older has been accelerating faster than the divorce rate for any other age group. In the last forty years or so, we've done such a good job of training wives to be mothers and husbands to be breadwinners that by the time their children leave home, they've forgotten how to be partners.

By no means am I ignoring realities. Children must be attended to and money must be made. I'm simply saying that wives can, and should, remain wives first and foremost, even after they become mothers. Likewise, husbands can, and should, remain husbands first and foremost, regardless of the demands of their careers. Mother, father, breadwinner—these are all secondary roles. Husband and wife are the primary adult roles in the family. If all of this is somewhat difficult to accept, it's only because the cultural program to which I referred earlier is so demanding and insistent, so powerful and persuasive, that we succumb to it without thinking through the consequences.

The bad news is that many American families are in trouble because husbands and wives have lost touch with their primary commitment. The good news is that this problem is easier to fix than it is to live with. You can begin by giving your marriage some quality time.

The Real Meaning of Quality Time

The concept of quality time was coined in the early 1970s to address the anxieties of mothers who feared they were doing their children harm by entering, or re-entering, the workplace.

"Not so!" announced the purveyors of quality time. "It isn't necessary that you spend a lot of time with your children as long as the time you spend is of good quality."

True enough, but your average American working mom takes that to mean she's obliged to spend every free moment giving her children large, compensatory doses of positive attention. So, after picking up the children from the day-care center, she goes home and flogs herself with the quality time "whip" until it's time for the children to go to bed, by which point Mom's too burned out to put anything of quality into the marriage. If Dad joined in the fun, he's burned out, too. If he didn't, he's either too numb from watching television or too stressed out from working on stuff he brought home from the office to be much of a husband.

The fact is, leaving a child in someone else's care for significant periods of time isn't inherently bad unless you leave the child with the wrong people or in the wrong kind of place. For this reason, it's important that parents research their child-care options thoroughly and choose on the basis of quality, rather than hype, convenience, or cost.

If, while you work, your child is being taken good care of by big people who are trained to take good care of little people, and who understand their needs, then you have nothing for which to feel guilty and nothing for which to compensate. If, from

Monday through Friday, you have only three or four hours a day in which to be a family, that's all the more reason to keep your family priorities in clear focus during that time.

I'm thinking about a young couple whom I saw several years ago concerning their four-year-old daughter's apparent need to always be the center of attention. These parents were besieged by a steady stream of disruptions and interruptions, all of which were variations on the theme of "Look at me!" If they didn't immediately attend to their daughter's demands, she began whining. If that didn't bring results, she'd begin jumping up and down, flapping her hands and crying. An absolutely ludicrous sight, to be sure, but one that can be rather frightening, especially for inexperienced parents.

These parents, both of whom worked, felt trapped between a rock and a hard place. On the one hand, even though their daughter was in one of the best day-care programs in the city, they felt their dual careers were depriving her of much-needed time and attention. Her constant demands for attention, they theorized, were expressions of insecurity. Unfortunately, dual careers were not an option. At this point in the life of the family, they were an economic necessity.

"So what can we do?" they asked.

"First," I said, "tell me what you're *already* doing."

"Well," said the wife, "when we get home, we more or less devote ourselves to her. We play with her, we read to her, we take her for walks. After being away from us all day, we feel she deserves to have us all to herself."

"Stop right there," I said. "I think we've located the problem."

I proceeded to tell this young couple about some friends of mine, both of whom have careers. They also have two school-age children. After school, the kids are transported to a day-care center where they stay until shortly after five o'clock, when their father picks them up and brings them home.

Several years ago, my friends created a rather unusual rule: For thirty minutes after everyone gets home, the children are not allowed in the den, kitchen, or any other room where their parents happen to be. They can play in their rooms or, weather permitting, go outside. The parents take this time to unwind and talk as they prepare the evening meal.

Until they created the thirty-minute rule, my friends had felt obliged to devote themselves to their children through the entire evening. The more attention they gave the children, however, the more demanding, self-centered, and disobedient the children became. Eventually, and not a moment too soon, my friends realized that the kids had taken over the family. In pursuit of good parenting, they'd created a monster!

Realizing that their relationship with one another was more important than their relationship with their children, they moved their marriage back to center-stage in the family. The thirty-minute rule was one of many major policy changes. Here's how it worked: After everyone had arrived home in the evening, my friends set the stove timer for thirty minutes and directed the children to find things to do. When the children tested the new rule, the parents refused their request and sent them packing, firmly but gently. For the first few weeks, as soon as the kids heard the timer go off, they'd come racing into the kitchen, eager to get some parental devotion. As time passed, the interval between the buzzer and the children's appearance began to lengthen. Eventually, setting the timer became unnecessary. The children came home and found things to do until supper. After the meal, they'd return to their play until nearly bedtime, when they'd ask for a story and a proper tucking-in.

I would describe these children as independent, secure, outgoing, happy, mature, playful, obedient, polite . . . need I go on? Their parents cured them of their addiction to attention by putting the marriage first. In so doing, they defied a whole set of "shoulds" that operate in many, if not most, dual-career families.

The little girl's parents were sufficiently impressed by my story to try my friends' technique for themselves. I lost touch with them for about six months and then happened to run into them one day in a store. They apologized for not having gotten back in touch with me, but said there hadn't been a need. As we exchanged pleasantries, I could tell that things were different in their family. For one thing, the little girl stood quietly next to her parents without interrupting our conversation.

"We tried the thirty-minute rule," they said, "and it worked! These days, after we all get home, Julie takes responsibility for entertaining herself. We talk during dinner, but afterward, she finds things to do until it's time for bed. At that point, we spend about thirty minutes reading and talking until lights out. We're all a lot happier these days." And looking down at her daughter, this young mother asked, "Aren't we, Julie?" Julie looked up, first at her mother, then at me. Smiling, she nodded and gave me a great, big hug.

I love happy endings, don't you?

More Quality Time

Here are several more ways of making quality time for the marriage as well as helping children understand that Mom and Dad's relationship is Numero Uno. (Single parents: These apply to you, too!)

—Don't allow children to interrupt your conversations. Make them wait their turn, preferably in another room. Say, "We'll let you know when we're finished talking." A child who simply "can't wait" probably needs five minutes of "cool down" in his or her room.

—Create a weekly "Parents' Night Out" and don't let anything except acts of God interfere with the commitment. Every now and then, go off for a weekend without the kids. They need to realize that the marriage is a separate, autonomous entity within the family; that it has a life, and needs, of its own.

—Put children to bed early. Remember that your children's bedtime is for *your* benefit. In other words, determine how much "down" time you need in the evening during which you have no childrearing responsibilities and set bedtimes accordingly. Instead of putting children to bed when *they're* ready, put them to bed when *you're* ready to hang up your roles as mom and dad and just be husband and wife. I've always felt that 8:30 is late enough for preschoolers; 9:00 for children of grade-school age. I recommend that older children be in their rooms no later than 9:30, particularly on school nights. If children are willing to "make themselves invisible," it's all right if they read or work on hobbies until a slightly later light's out.

—Once the kids are in bed, reduce distractions that interfere with communication and intimacy. Agree not to do either housework or office work after the kids' bedtime. Spend this time getting back in touch with the feelings that led to your original commitment. In this regard, the worst possible, least creative thing you can do is get in the habit of centering your time together in the evenings around television.

Watching Television Alone

Since the early 1950s, the divorce rate in the United States has climbed steadily. Interestingly enough, it was in the early fifties that television invaded the American home and began dominating the life of the American family, especially in the evening. In your average American family, the television is on six hours a day, or forty-two hours a week. In a recent poll, couples married for one year were asked to identify their most prized household possession. Not surprisingly, most of the people in the survey named their televisions. These couples were also asked what single aspect of their marriage needed the greatest amount of improvement. Ironically, and sadly, the majority answered "communication."

Another recent study found that the average American couple engages in less than thirty minutes of meaningful, one-to-one conversation in a week's time. Each of those two people, however, is likely to spend more than twenty hours a week staring at a television set.

The language of television watching conceals its reality. People talk about watching television "together," but the two things—watching television and togetherness—are mutually exclusive. When a family gathers in front of a television, each individual becomes isolated in his or her own audio-visual tunnel. You may as well be twenty miles away from the person sitting next to you if you're both staring at what is deservedly referred to as "the boob tube." You can't watch television and truly communicate or be intimate at the same time. It's either one or the other. Ask yourselves, what's more important?

Questions?

Q: I'm a single mother with two children. How does what you've said about putting the marriage first apply to single parents like myself?

A: The situation may be different, but the priorities aren't. In a two-parent family, the needs of the marriage must come first. In a single-parent family, the needs of the single parent must come first.

The single-parent "trap" is more likely to snare single mothers than single fathers. For a number of reasons, mothers are more likely than fathers to neglect their own needs in the course of meeting their children's. Mothers also have more difficulty making the distinction between what their children truly need and what they simply want. When single mothers have primary custody of their children, which is most often the case, they often feel that they need to overcompensate for the absence of a father in the home. In the process, the fall into the trap of overindulging and overprotecting the children, and wind up stretching their emotional resources to the breaking point.

Look at it this way: You can't supply anyone else's "warehouse" unless your own is fully stocked. But instead of taking care of themselves well enough to keep their warehouses full, single mothers often feel compelled to forgo their own needs in favor of their children's. They give and give—both emotionally and materially—to children who begin taking this giving for granted and appreciate it less and less. In no time at all, the children are likely to begin acting like demanding, ungrateful brats. Eventually and inevitably, the single mother's ability to go on giving collapses, and she vents her frustration at her children. Then guilt sets in.

"I shouldn't have gotten so mad at the kids. It's not *their* fault there's only one parent in the home."

At this point, our single mother feels compelled to do something special for her children in order to make up for having lost her temper at them. And it's back to business as usual.

In this continuing soap opera, the children are victims of circumstance, and Mom must do penance through self-sacrifice. Every time she gets angry at her kids, she ends up feeling like a bad parent. "If I could only control my temper," she thinks, "everything would be okay." But her temper's not the problem. It's her *lack* of temper. To solve the problem, she has to learn to temper her own needs with those of her children. She must temper her giving to her children and begin getting for herself.

Compensations never work. Instead of solving problems, they eventually become part of them. As a single mother, you must establish an identity for yourself that has nothing to do with your kids. You must allow the adult woman in you to separate herself from her role as "Mom" and get her needs—social, vocational, recreational, and sexual—met. In short, for your children's sake as well as your own, you must give yourself permission to be creatively selfish. Only then will you have "inventory" enough to share freely with your kids.

Q: I'm a single mother with two children, ages six and four. Their father and I have been divorced for over a year, and I've been involved in a serious relationship for the last six months. Unfortunately, the children don't seem to like my boyfriend. He's bent over backwards to win them over, but the harder he tries, the less they seem to care. On more than one occasion, they've made it clear they don't want him over. The four-year-old has even told him, "It's time for you to go home now." I couldn't believe it! We're talking about marriage, but the children's attitude toward him gives me doubts. How should I handle this? Also, when is it all right to begin showing affection to one another around them?

A: Actually, although the "It's time for you to go home now" statement was fairly outrageous, it's typical of the things kids say under circumstances such as these. Not having learned the art of social diplomacy, young children can be rudely candid when things don't suit them.

Keep in mind that their "dislike" of your boyfriend isn't really personal. In their eyes, Dad has a continuing interest in the family. Your boyfriend's presence in the home, therefore, evokes a strong protective response from the kids.

Consider, also, that from Dad's leaving to the time your boyfriend arrived on the scene, the children enjoyed your undivided attention. They're probably having difficulty accepting the fact that some of those "goodies" are now going to someone else. This doesn't mean, however, that you should give them *more* attention. It means they need to adjust to getting *less*.

Talk to them about their feelings. Acknowledge that what they're experiencing is normal and help them understand that it's not really your boyfriend they don't like, but the situation. Ask for their cooperation in extending hospitality and courtesy to any and all of your guests. An open discussion of this sort, in which you give the children an opportunity to express themselves and are accepting of their feelings, may or may not solve the problem. If it doesn't, then you'll have to get more assertive.

Confront any further displays of rudeness on the spot. Tell the children, in no uncertain terms, that they do not have permission to be rude. Then banish them to their rooms until they decide to apologize. If you're consistent with this, the problem should disappear from view in fairly short order.

To help the kids adjust to seeing you and your boyfriend be affectionate toward one another, take things one step at a time. First, let them see you holding hands. If they try to break you apart, put them in their place and go on holding. When they seem to accept hand-holding, you can go "public" with hugging and kissing.

It would also help if your boyfriend made gestures of affection toward the children. He might, for instance, offer to read to them. If you're on an outing and one of them gets tired, he might offer to carry. Eventually, he can help you put the kids to bed. Again, don't rush it. Be sensitive to the children's "comfort zone." If your boyfriend extends an invitation to the kids, and they turn him down, he shouldn't take it personally. He should just step back, regroup, and try later. Patience is the most important factor here.

If you and your boyfriend are hugging and the kids try to "get in on the act," let them know it's not "their turn." This says that your relationship with your boyfriend is, at times, exclusive. If you eventually decide to get married, this precedent will help you put the marriage at the center of the family.

Q: I'm a married working woman with a six-week-old baby girl. Before she was born, I had planned on returning to work after three months. Now that she's here, however, I'm beginning to feel I should be with her more than my job will allow. Is it psychologically damaging for a baby to be separated from its mother for long periods of time? When is the ideal time for a mother to return to work if her job isn't financially necessary?

A: Bonding studies suggest that lots of parent-child interaction during infancy is necessary to healthy development, psychological and otherwise. Burton White, author of *The First Three Years of Life,* contends that children should, for the most part, be taken care of by their parents until age three. He recommends against full-time day care until then. Other developmental psychologists agree there is no truly adequate parent substitute during the first few months of life, but don't feel there's any real danger to leaving older babies and toddlers with competent, attentive secondary care-givers, such as in-home sitters and trained day-care staff.

Ideally, parents should take primary care of their children for at least the first year of their children's lives. Realistically, however, if that's not possible because of economic pressures, or you truly feel your own mental health is at stake, stay home for at least six weeks and then go back to work. Regardless of when you decide to return to your job, it's important that you choose quality care. For example, a day-care center's child/staff ratio should be low enough to ensure each child adequate individual attention. For infants, the ratio should be no greater than five-to-one.

Some of the questions parents should ask when shopping for child care are: Does the center require prior formal training and certification of key staff persons, or are they hired "off the street?" Does the center have enough play materials to go around, and are they of sufficient variety? Does it have a safe, interesting outdoor play area? What are its discipline policies?

Most states have an office within the Department of Human

Services that oversees the delivery of child-care services. They will be glad to provide parents with information and referral concerning child-care resources.

Q: Is it true, as many people seem to feel, that mothers are more important than fathers to the childrearing process?

A: We fathers are *just* as important as mothers to the raising of children. Unfortunately, the average American still *acts* as if childrearing is primarily "woman's work." As a result, there is a general tendency to ignore or minimize the strengths fathers can, and do, bring to the parenting process.

The result of this lopsided state of affairs is that mothers tend to feel more responsible for their children than they actually are, while fathers often feel insignificant and even excluded. Worse yet, some fathers use this myth as a convenient excuse to exclude themselves. In effect, many American mothers, even though married and living with their spouses, function as single parents.

To be sure, there are predictable differences in the ways mothers *versus* fathers relate to and interact with their children. These differences have to do with biology, psychology, cultural expectations, and practical considerations. For example, in all cultures and in all times, mothers have occupied the role of primary parent during infancy and early childhood. This arrangement makes sense from several perspectives, including the fact that women have the built-in ability to feed their babies, while fathers do not.

But primary need not, and should not, mean exclusive. Even during the early years, fathers are important. Studies have shown, for example, that preschoolers whose fathers are actively involved in their upbringing tend to be more outgoing, adaptable, and accepting of challenge. Other research indicates that children with involved fathers do better in school, get along better with peers, and have better self-esteem. Children of actively involved, interested fathers are also less likely, during their teens, to become pregnant and/or develop problems with drugs and/or alcohol.

In *Never Cry Wolf,* naturalist/author Farley Mowat gives an insightful look at the wolf family, one of the few monogamous family units in the animal kingdom. Wolf cubs are never far from their mother. She protects and nurtures them until they reach adolescence, at which point the male wolf takes over as primary parent. He teaches his offspring to hunt and kill and survive in an often hostile environment. In other words, the wolf-father endows his children with the skills they will need for self-sufficiency.

Reading Mowat's book, the thought struck me that perhaps we humans would do well to take a lesson from the wolf. I'm convinced, in fact, that children need more "mothering" than "fathering" during infancy and early childhood. I'm equally convinced that as children grow and their needs for autonomy increase, fathers become increasingly important.

I can already hear the outcry: "Rosemond's a chauvinist! He's saying that, by themselves, women aren't capable of raising successful children!"

No, I'm not a chauvinist. I'm a realist. I'm saying that women are inherently better suited to certain aspects of parenting than fathers and *vice versa*. I'm saying that their respective strengths are better suited to certain areas and times of a child's development than others. In the real world, mothers and fathers contribute differently, but equally, to their children's "wholeness." I'm saying children fare better with two parents working together than with one of either sex working alone. This is not to say that single parents can't do a good job of raising children. Please note that I didn't say "two parents," but "two parents *working together*."

Nor am I saying that all fathers would be wonderful dads if only given the chance. It's a father's responsibility to create opportunities for creative relationships with his children. If he doesn't, it sure as shootin' isn't their momma's fault.

¶

Q: My husband and I were both married in our mid-thirties and now, five years later, have a two-year-old boy. We've tentatively decided not to have any more children. To be perfectly frank, we just don't have the energy for another baby at this stage of the game. We'd like to know whether you have any particular concerns and/or recommendations regarding only children.

A: There are several caution flags I raise with parents of only children.

First, because all the parents' "eggs," so to speak, are in one basket, the only child tends to receive more attention and more things than he would if he were in a family of two or more children. If the attention is excessive, it is to the disadvantage of all concerned, but particularly to the child. As I pointed out earlier, too much attention is addictive and detrimental to the growth of independence and self-esteem.

Overindulgence also leads to behaviors typically associated with the "spoiled" child—making unreasonable demands, acting "starved" for attention, throwing tantrums, disrespect, and disobedience.

The prevailing childrearing myth of the sixties and seventies was that children need a lot of attention from parents. Except for the first few years of life, this simply isn't true. Children need attention, but too much can create a dependency that stifles emotional growth and development.

A second caution addresses something I've often heard from parents of only children: "It was just easier to take him with us everywhere we went." On the surface of things, this degree of parent-child closeness may look desirable, but in the final analysis, it is not. As a result of being included in so many adult activities, the child begins to perceive the marriage as a *threesome*, centered around him. This family dynamic makes it difficult, if not impossible, for the child to outgrow his infantile self-centeredness. Also, to the degree a child is treated and regards himself as an equal, parents will have a difficult time establishing themselves as authority figures. Furthermore, because the boundary between the child and the marriage is blurred, the child may fail to develop a clear sense of his own identity.

The "only-child syndrome" breeds its share of behavior problems. They typically include interrupting adult conversations, demanding to be included in adult activities, problems separating from parents, wanting "in on the action" any time parents show affection toward one another, disobedience, disrespect, and wanting to constantly be the center of attention.

Despite the bickering that often characterizes sibling relationships, siblings help each other learn to share and resolve conflict. Only children sometimes have problems in both these areas. With other children, they tend to be possessive of their belongings and want everything to go their way. These potential problems are made worse by the fact that, by virtue of being included in so many adult activities, the only child is often better socialized to adults than to peers. Consequently, the only child is often perceived by peers as having a superior, "know-it-all" attitude.

A little foresight can prevent these problems from ever developing:

—Center the family around the marriage, not the child.

—Limit the child's inclusion in adult activities.

—Enroll the child in day care no later than age three.

—Avoid indulging the child with either too much attention or too many things.

Q: What suggestions do you have for the parents of a five-year-old only child who is addicted to attention, television, and toys? He is very demanding and easily bored. Instead of playing with other children in the neighborhood, he either wants us to play with him or wants to watch television. If we go somewhere, he either goes with us or stays with grandparents. We want to undo the damage we've done, but aren't sure where to begin or how quickly to go about doing it.

A: To begin with, you haven't done any permanent damage. You've simply set certain precedents that aren't working to anyone's advantage. You need to dismantle and replace them with more workable ones. Making major changes of this sort demands a well-organized, strategic approach. If you're ready, here are some tips on getting started.

First, limit your son's television watching to no more than thirty minutes a day. The more time children spend occupied with television, the less able they are to find creative ways of occupying themselves. By turning the television off, you force him to find other ways of using his time. At first, he'll want you to occupy it for him, so . . .

Limit the amount of time you spend playing with him to two, fifteen-minute periods a day, once in the morning and once in the afternoon. When he asks you to play with him, set the kitchen timer for fifteen minutes. When it rings, excuse yourself and go back to what you were doing. This doesn't mean you're at his beck and call twice daily. If he asks you at an inconvenient time, tell him he's going to have to wait. If he pesters or whines, send him to his room for fifteen minutes.

Third, stop taking him with you everywhere you go. When you go out, leave him with baby-sitters instead of always with relatives. Find a teenager in your neighborhood who relates well to children and hire her/him to come into your home one night a week while you and your husband go out to dinner or a movie. The understanding that he isn't a member of the marriage will help your son develop independence and a clear sense of personal identity. In the long run, it is also a prerequisite to successful emancipation.

Fourth, reduce his toy inventory. A child this age should have very few store-bought toys, and those should consist primarily of "flexible" toy sets such as Lincoln Logs, Tinker Toys, and Legos. Where toys are concerned, I often tell parents that if the toy wasn't in production prior to 1955, it's probably not worth buying. The right toys, in small number, encourage initiative, resourcefulness, and creativity.

Prepare him for all this by sitting him down one evening and telling him, in a gentle but straightforward manner, about the changes you're about to make. If he asks why, just say, "This is what happens when children are five years old." A more involved explanation will only confuse him and/or make him feel like there's something wrong with him.

Later, if he balks at some new way of doing things, you can simply say, "Remember the talk we had? This is one of the changes we were talking about."

By the way, it's really not necessary that you do this one step at a time. In fact, your son will adjust more quickly to the changes if you implement them all at once.

Q: I am a single mother with a nine-year-old son. My ex-husband and I divorced when Robbie was three. I've recently decided to get married again. My fiancé, who has been married before but has no children, and I have been seeing each other for almost two years. He and Robbie have a good relationship, which was one of the things I considered before saying "yes." What are some of the problems we may face in our new family?

A: You and your husband-to-be are creating what's known as a "stepfamily"—a family in which one parent is a stepparent.

The stepfamily is the most rapidly growing family type in America, representing 15 percent of our nation's families. Nearly twenty million children live in stepfamilies and another million are added every year. At this rate, the stepfamily will eventually replace the traditional family as the dominant American family type.

There are actually two types of stepfamilies: The primary stepfamily and the secondary stepfamily. The primary stepfamily includes the parent who has primary custody of the children. The children visit with, but do not reside with, the secondary stepfamily. Since most mothers retain custody of their children after divorce, most primary stepfamilies are headed by a mother and stepfather.

The primary stepfamily faces a set of problems that are different from those faced by the traditional family. The two biggest hurdles involve first, the need to establish the marriage at the center of the family, and second, the need to establish the stepfather as an authority figure.

Unfortunately, in many, if not most, stepfamily situations, certain precedents have been set prior to the remarriage that interfere with the accomplishment of these goals.

The first of these involves the fact that, following divorce, a mother becomes a single parent. Because she has no spouse, her relationship with her children may become the most important relationship in her life. Increasingly, the single mother devotes herself to the raising of her children, and her children become increasingly dependent upon her attention. In effect, an unwritten "pact" evolves which essentially reads, "You meet my needs, and I'll meet yours."

Enter boyfriend, who quickly perceives the strength of the mother-child relationship and adopts an "if you can't beat 'em, join 'em" attitude. Wittingly or unwittingly, he begins to court not only the mother, but her children as well. He tries to become their friend, a good buddy. He correctly realizes that he must, in effect, obtain the children's approval if he stands a chance of having their mother accept his proposal of marriage.

After the remarriage takes place, everyone continues to cling to old habits which, unfortunately, no longer work. The mother has difficulty moving out of a primary relationship with her children and into a primary relationship with her spouse. As a result, the stepfather begins to feel like a "third wheel."

Making matters worse is the fact that the stepfather's need to shift gears from "good buddy" to parent causes everyone anxiety, confusion, and even anger. He attempts to discipline and the children run to their mother, complaining that he's being "mean." She responds protectively, accusing him of overreacting and/or taking his "jealousy" out on the kids. And 'round and 'round they start to go, and where they stop, heaven knows.

All this can be avoided, or at least minimized, if people planning stepfamilies will, above all else, remember two things:

—First, the marriage *must* be the most important relationship in the family. Stepfamilies are no different from other families in this respect.

—Second, the stepparent *must* assume authority equal to that of the natural parent. This means, of course, that the natural parent must be willing to share authority equally with his or her new spouse.

An ounce of prevention is always better than a pound of cure. Take the time to discuss just exactly what you're going to do to avoid these problems, and how you're going to handle them when and if they come up.

Q: How should a husband and wife handle arguments between them when the children are around? We do our best not to argue in front of our two children, ages seven and four, but occasionally we let one slip when they're within earshot. It always seems to bother them, which makes us feel guilty. In fact, the younger one has sometimes told us point-blank to "Stop!" When this happens, which isn't often, we stop and apologize to them. Since neither of us ever heard our parents argue, we don't feel secure in this area of our relationship with our children. Do you have any suggestions?

33

A: First of all, I suggest you start letting your children hear some of your arguments. Second, I advise that you *never* allow them to interrupt while you're in the midst of one.

Disagreement is a natural, inevitable aspect of human relationships. As intimacy within a relationship increases, so does the likelihood of disagreement. You can't have marriage without disagreement, but you can have marriage without *argument*, which is the confrontation and working through of disagreement. Unfortunately, when two people don't confront the disagreements they inevitably face once they're married, their relationship stands a good chance of never growing. It's too bad your parents never taught you the facts of being married. Don't make the same mistake.

Your children need to learn, first, that arguments come with marriage. Then they need to learn that arguments don't destroy people. Finally, they need to learn how to engage in constructive disagreement with other people. If they don't learn these things from you, from whom are they going to learn them?

I said your children should hear *some* of your arguments. Obviously, there are certain topics children should *not* overhear their parents discussing, whether they're arguing or not. If you want them to learn that arguments aren't necessarily destructive, you are responsible for conducting your disagreements in a civilized, constructive manner. This doesn't mean you can't raise your voices, but it does mean you should not slander or belittle one another. You give respect to one another's point of view through active listening, making an attempt to consider points of view other than the two you brought to the discussion, and trying to reach a win-win resolution.

There will undoubtedly be times when you will want to save your disagreements for after the children are asleep. But there are probably more times when you want to have your disagreements when they're awake and perhaps even in the same room. If you choose to have an argument in front of them and they attempt to interrupt you, you should say something like, "We are simply disagreeing with one another. If you don't like it, you may leave the room. If you stay, you may not interrupt us or cry. If you do, we'll send you to your rooms until our discussion is over."

If you start arguing and the children suddenly appear in the room with you, it's because they want to make sure everything is going to be all right. Reassure them that you're both alive and well and intend to stay that way, and send them from the room.

Q: My husband and I are expecting our first child in November and are already having a disagreement over names—ours, not the baby's. My husband's older brother—whom he hero-worships—and sister-in-law allow their two children to call them by their first names. Now my husband says he wants our child to call us by our first names. I simply cannot envision our son or daughter calling us "Jim" and "Linda," but my husband says "Mom" and "Dad" are roles that prevent give-and-take in the parent-child relationship and get in the way of open communication.

A: This disagreement over what your child will call you is more significant than it may sound. It says that the two of you are on completely different wavelengths regarding your attitudes toward parenthood.

Furthermore, since your attitudes and conduct as parents will have great influence on your relationship as husband and wife, your marriage stands a good chance of ending up on the rocks if you don't do something now to get your act together. For that reason, I think the two of you would be wise to consider some marriage counseling before the baby comes.

Your husband's reluctance to accept, without reservation, the role of "Dad" suggests that perhaps there were serious problems in his relationship with his parents, and particularly his father. Were his parents rigid and unaffectionate? Were they abusive, emotionally or otherwise? Did one or both of his parents have a drinking problem? During his childhood, was the older brother more of a "father" than the father actually was?

If the answer to any of these questions is "Yes," then I'd also recommend that your husband find a therapist who can help him work through the confusion and hurt of his childhood. He needs to realize that having your child call him "Jim" as opposed to "Dad" is a compensation, not a solution, for problems he experienced with his parents. As such, it could have disastrous results.

As parents, the two of you will be responsible for giving

your child a balance of love and firm discipline. In so doing, you guarantee your child's security and self-esteem, not to mention his or her love and respect for you. Your husband's belief that "Mom" and "Dad" are roles that prevent give-and-take and interfere with communication needs to be addressed now.

"Mom" and "Dad" are terms which should embody both endearment and respect. By contrast, "Jim" and "Linda" convey neither endearment nor respect. For a child to call his parents by their first names implies that the relationship is democratic. This is fine between friends, but the parent-child relationship is not and cannot be democratic. When parents attempt, through obvious or subtle means, to create the illusion of democracy in the family, the outcome is chaos.

"Mom" and "Dad" are also associated, almost automatically, with emotional responses—trust, belongingness, and the like—that are valuable, even essential, to a healthy parent-child relationship, one that fosters security and good self-esteem.

I would guess that herein lies part of the problem. "Mom" and "Dad" evoke painful, rather than nurturing, memories for your husband—memories he would prefer to avoid. I heartily encourage him to explore his feelings in more detail and in more depth, preferably with a qualified therapist.

Q: A local television talk show recently featured a pediatrician who wrote a book on fussy babies. The doctor's description of what he called a "high-need baby" fit my six-month-old to a T. He is very active, alert, and requires a great deal of stimulation and attention. If I put him down for even a moment, he begins screaming. I'm beginning to feel I no longer have a life of my own. According to this doctor, I should "wear the baby like a sweater." When the interviewer pointed out that this leaves no room for other responsibilities, the doctor replied that meeting the baby's needs was more important than doing housework or anything else. Do you agree or disagree?

A: I agree with the doctor's description of "high-need infants." It's also true that if you repeatedly frustrate an infant's needs for closeness and attention, you're going to delay the development of independence and create a host of other potentially serious problems.

I *don't* agree, however, with the doctor's statement that parents of high-need babies should "wear them like a sweater." That's similar to saying "You can't spoil an infant," which, while essentially true, doesn't mean parents should pick up a baby every time he or she cries. That's not only impractical, especially with a chronically fussy baby, but also unnecessary.

Meeting your baby's needs involves meeting your own as well. Stated differently, you can't take good care of someone else unless you also take equally good care of yourself. Parents who feel they must devote themselves exclusively to their babies and forget about themselves eventually begin feeling frustrated and resentful. If there's one thing a baby *doesn't* need, it's parents who feel that parenthood is a burden.

Somewhere between the doctor's injunction that you wear your baby like a sweater and a state of totally selfish neglect, there's a point of balance where it's possible for you to meet both *your* needs *and* your child's. There's no getting around the fact that fussy, high-need infants require more attention and physical closeness than the norm. And, for the most part, it's good practice to respond to an infant's cries shortly after they begin. However, even if he cries, there's no harm in putting your baby down for a few minutes to take care of something you can't do if you're holding him.

In other words, if it's practical for you to "wear him like a sweater," do so. If it's not, put him down and do what you must. If you leave the room, keep talking to him or at least call to him every ten seconds or so. The sound of your voice may not stop him from crying, but at least he'll know you're still there, somewhere. Besides, there's only one way he's going to learn that you aren't going to abandon him, and that's if you occasionally put him down, do what you have to do, and then come back.

A couple of things are going to happen within the next few months that will make life with your baby a whole lot easier. First, he's going to become increasingly mobile. At the moment, his need to explore is thwarted by the fact that he can't get around on his own. So, you do his exploring for him. You bring things to him, thus feeding his curiosity. Right now, you have to do a lot of "entertaining," because a high-need baby doesn't stay interested in any one thing for very long. The more mobile he gets, however, the less he's going to depend on you for stimulation, and the more time you'll have for yourself.

Second, around age eight months, he's going to develop what's called "object permanence." Right now, in his mind, if something vanishes from sight, it no longer exists. That includes you! In a few months, however, he'll begin realizing that you're here to stay, and he'll be able to tolerate your being out of sight for longer and longer periods of time.

Until then, feel free to put him down and go to the bathroom, brush your teeth, wash your face, boil water, fix yourself something to eat, or just sit and pull your wits together for a few minutes. Fear not, despite the good doctor's warnings, you won't cause permanent psychological scars.

Q: What do you think about letting children sleep with their parents?

A: Generally speaking, children should sleep in their own rooms, in their own beds. I would, under certain circumstances, however, bend this rule. For example, there's no harm in having *infants* sleep in the same room with their parents. No harm, either, in letting children come temporarily into their parents' beds during illness or periods of extreme stress, such as might follow a significant death or a house fire. But aside from exceptions such as these, I say, "Children to their own beds at a reasonably early hour!"

Sleeping in his or her own bed helps establish that the child is an independent, autonomous individual, with a clearly separate identity. In addition, parents sleeping together and separate from the child enhances the child's view of the marriage as not only a separate entity within the family, but also the most important relationship within the family. A child who sleeps with his or her parents is in danger of never reaching this understanding, of feeling wrongly that the marriage is a threesome.

Separate sleeping arrangements also sets an important precedent regarding separation. Children who separate from their parents at bedtime are better prepared to separate from them under other circumstances—when sitters come, at day care, the first day of school, for swimming lessons, and so on.

Q: But isn't it true that the custom of having children sleep separate from their parents only began around the turn of this century? Isn't it also true that before this and since prehistoric times, children were kept in bed with, or at least in another bed beside, their parents? If so, it would then seem that whether society condones it or not, letting children sleep with parents is more natural than making children sleep alone.

A: I'm absolutely certain that my position rests on firm clinical and developmental ground, as opposed to simply being an extension of societal expectations and prejudices.

Regarding the historical antecedents of this issue, I think I'm correct in saying that in other cultures and in other times, children have slept with their parents only when there were no other options. For instance, it would have been impractical, perhaps even deadly, for our prehistoric ancestors to hold out for nothing less than a two-bedroom cave. Nor does it make sense for nomadic people to lug two-bedroom tents from site to site, or Eskimos to waste valuable time and energy building two-bedroom igloos. In this and other countries, where you find parents and children sleeping together, it's usually out of necessity rather than choice.

Furthermore, the fact that a certain childrearing practice is or was common to more primitive cultures may qualify it as more "natural," but "natural" and healthy are not necessarily one and the same.

I'm sure that the characteristics of the particular culture dictate how this issue will be handled. In cultures where children usually sleep with their parents, there have no doubt evolved other ways of "cutting the cord." The adolescent puberty rites of some native cultures would be a prime example. In Western cultures, however, the separation of child and parents at bedtime is, I'm convinced, crucial to the development of autonomy—the child's *and* the parents'.

Q: I'm thirty-eight and have been happily married for five years.

I'm undecided over whether or not to have children. At times, I think a child would be wonderful, especially in our later years. On the other hand, I have no overwhelming desire to spend the next eighteen years raising a child. What questions should my husband and I ask ourselves to help us reach this decision?

A: Your dilemma is becoming increasingly commonplace. More and more people are putting off marriage as well as the decision to have or not have children. Considering that this is an extremely emotional issue, it's admirable that you're taking the time to weigh the pros and cons patiently and rationally.

It's unfortunate that our culture continues to communicate to women that they are in some way *incomplete* unless they opt for motherhood. Instead of enjoying the process of raising children, many women pressure themselves to "perform" at it. In order to demonstrate what good and conscientious mothers they are, they wind up devoting themselves body and soul to self-centered children who don't know their limits, never learn to accept "No" for an answer, and take everything they get for granted.

So, just because two married people are *capable* of having children doesn't mean they *should*. The beauty of being human is that each of us is gifted with a broad range of capabilities. If you feel inspired to raise children, then by all means raise children. On the other hand, if you'd rather raise sheep, then raise sheep.

Ask yourselves these questions:

—Are we *both* in favor of having children or does one of us harbor reservations? When, instead of being mutually arrived at, the decision to have children is made for the "sake of" one of the two adults involved, the eventual toll on the marriage can be enough to destroy it.

—Do we want to be just finishing our childrearing responsibilities around age sixty, or would we rather spend our middle years together, relatively free to come, go, and do as we please?

—Do we feel emotionally up to dealing with the loss of freedom and the long-term obligations, financial and otherwise, that come with raising children?

—Do we enjoy being around other people's children or do they tend to annoy us?

—Did we have happy childhoods? I find that people tend to enjoy raising children to about the same extent they enjoyed *being* children. A happy childhood is perhaps the best guarantee of a happy parenthood.

You should also consider that the potential for certain genetic problems increases with the ages of the parents. Are you willing to take the higher risk of having a handicapped child? If you want more information about these dangers, ask your OB-GYN to refer you to a genetic counselor.

A Final Word

Healing and strengthening the nucleus of your family, your marriage—or, if single, your own life—is something you can start doing *right now.* And once you've started, it's something you'll need to keep doing every day. Put your marriage first, and it's more likely to last. If you're a single parent, put *yourself* first and you'll soon find you have far more of yourself to give to your children.

POINT TWO

The Voice of Authority

A question I'm often asked by parents is, "John, how can we get our children to obey us?"

My answer is simple and direct: "If you *expect* your children to obey, they will."

At this, parents will often look puzzled and then say something like, "But, John, we *do* expect our children to obey us, but they *don't*! Instead, they complain and argue. Getting them to do anything is a major hassle. So how can you tell us that if we simply *expect* obedience, it will magically happen?"

I'm sure most American parents would say that they expect their children to obey. I'm equally sure that most American children are not truly obedient. When told to do something by parents, the typical American child does not display a willing, cooperative attitude. Instead, he/she ignores, whines, argues, gets mad, talks back, and so on.

The once-upon-a-time "Yes, Sir," "No, Sir," obedient child has become virtually extinct. But this sorry state of affairs is not the fault of children. It's the fault of parents who beat forever around the bush of obedience, afraid to disturb any leaves, lest they damage the child's supposedly fragile psyche. It's the fault of parents who, instead of truly *expecting* children to obey, only go so far as *wishing* they would.

The distinction between expecting and wishing is found in the way parents communicate with children. When parents plead with children, they are wishing for obedience. When they complain to children about their behavior, they are wishing for obedience. When they bargain, bribe, threaten, give second chances, and "reason," they are wishing for obedience. Those are all relatively passive forms of wishing, but there are more active, and therefore less obvious, forms as well. For example, the parent who pounds on the table, gets red in the face, and threatens the recalcitrant child with bodily harm, is—appearances aside—actually *wishing* for obedience. You see, this parent is in a snit precisely because his wishes haven't come true.

By far the most common form of wishing takes place when parents argue with children. All arguments with children get started in one of two ways. In the first, the parent makes a decision which the child doesn't like, and the child strains forward, grimaces, and in a voice that sounds like fingernails being dragged across a chalkboard, screeches, *"Why!?"* In the second, parents make a decision which the child doesn't like and the child strains forward, grimaces, and in a voice that sounds like fingernails being dragged across a chalkboard, screeches, *"Why not!?"* Arguments start because parents make the mistake of thinking these are questions. They aren't! They are invitations to do battle. By accepting the invitation, you step squarely into quicksand. And the harder you struggle to be understood, the faster and farther you will sink.

A question is a request for information. If *"why!?"* and *"why not!?"* were truly questions, then two things would occur. First, the child would *listen* to your answer. Second, after having listened, the child would at least occasionally agree. Now think about it. When is the last time your child, after listening to your most eloquent, honest, sincere explanation, looked at you and said, "Well, gosh, Mom! Since you put it *that* way, I can't help but agree. Ah, gee, thanks for being my mom!"

What's that? It's never happened? Right! And it's never going to happen! Parents *cannot* win an argument with children. Winning an argument with someone means you change that person's way of thinking. As a result of the information or point of view you share, that person adopts a new and probably more mature point of view. Children don't have what it takes to appreciate and participate in this process. To compensate, they adopt an irrational position and hold on to it for dear life. So no matter how eloquent or how correct, parents cannot win because children can only see one point of view—their own.

Discussion requires the participation of two people who are as willing to listen as they are wanting to be heard. Children want to be heard, but they rarely want to listen. As the parent explains, the child waits for an opportunity to interrupt. But despite the obvious fact that attempting to explain the *"why!?"* or *"why not!?"* of a parental decision serves no purpose except the child's need to argue, parents continue to explain.

This is why I believe in the power of four particular words. As a child, I couldn't stand to hear these four words. They made me mad! So mad, in fact, that I promised myself I would *never* say them to my children. When I became a parent, I kept this promise for several years. Then, having brought myself to the brink of disaster, I woke up to reality and broke it. "Because I said so" became part of my parenting vocabulary.

Some people say that children have a *right* to know the reasons behind the decisions we make. I agree, but with certain amendments. Namely: They have a right to know in terms they can understand. Moreover, they have a right to know only if they are willing to listen. Finally, if the truth is "Because I said so," they have a right to know that, too.

Save Your Breath

I have a two-part rule governing the giving of explanations to children. It's called "The Save-Your-Breath Principle." Part One: Until a child is mature enough to understand a certain explanation, no amount of words will successfully convey that understanding. In that case, it is in the child's best interest for the parent to say "Because I said so" or words to that same effect. Part Two: When a child is old enough to understand the explanation, he's also old enough to figure it out on his own.

My two very strong-willed children frequently threw down the gauntlets of *"why!?"* and *"why not!?"* When they were young, and after I had recovered from my idealistic naiveté, I often answered them with "Because I said so." I didn't bark or sound exasperated. I simply looked them in the eye and said it, without hint of threat or apology. As they approached their teens, I switched over to something along the lines of "You know me well enough to answer that question on your own." In reply, they would scowl and sigh and say, "Oh, sure, you probably think that blah, blah, blah." Almost always, the "blah, blah, blah" was right on target, proving my point: They were old enough to figure out my reasons on their own. It also proved that, regardless, they weren't about to agree.

There were times when I *did* explain myself to my children, but *only* if they were willing to listen. If they weren't, which was often, especially during their early years, I would say, "I don't talk when people don't listen." With that, the explanation was either put on hold or permanently cancelled. If they protested loudly, I sent them to their rooms to cool down. Over the years, they learned that if they wanted to talk, they also had to listen. If they listened, I almost always ended up meeting them half way. In this manner, I tried to teach them that discussion, not argument, is the way to getting things accomplished in the world.

Some people don't like the idea of saying "Because I said so" to a child. They argue that it isn't a reason. I disagree. Not only is it a reason, it's often the *only* reason. Let's face it, most of the decisions parents make are arbitrary. They are matters of personal preference, not universal absolutes. Why, for example, must your child go to bed at eight o'clock when the neighbor's child, a year younger, is allowed to stay up until nine o'clock? Any and all attempts at explaining this inconsistency come down to simply this: "That's the way I want it." Why don't you allow your child to ride his bike past the corner, when his best friend can ride three blocks to the convenience store? Again, any and all explanations boil down to "That's just the way I want it." In other words, "Because I said so."

If those four words stick in your throat, try "Because this

decision belongs to me" or "Because I'm the parent and making decisions of this sort is my responsibility." If you feel you simply *must* give some manner of "correct" explanation, save your breath by trimming it to twenty-five words or less. Remember, however, that regardless of how carefully you phrase your answer, the child is not likely to agree. In fact, you just might want to preface your answer with, "Okay, I'll pretend you're really asking me a question, and I'll give you an answer. But I don't expect you to agree. On the other hand, don't expect me to change my mind." When the inevitable happens, say, "That's all right. As I said, I didn't expect you to agree. I'm also not changing my mind."

Family Government

In the late sixties and early seventies, several books were written on the subject of self-esteem in children. These books became the childrearing "bibles" of their day. Their authors maintained that children developed self-esteem only if their parents showed respect for them. Parents were to demonstrate respect for children by treating them as equals. This meant that parents were supposed to give children an equal voice in determining rules, chores, privileges, and so on. Compromise was the prescribed way of settling any and all differences of opinion. When a child misbehaved, parents were to appeal to the child's intellect and sense of responsibility by explaining the difference between right and wrong. Under no circumstances were parents to ever actually punish a child for misbehavior, because punishment violated the fundamental premise of equality.

These authors maintained that the only psychologically healthy family was a democratic family. In a democratic family, they said, no one was more powerful than anyone else. They marketed what they called "The Art of Active Listening," which essentially prohibited parents from telling children what to do. Instead, parents were to listen nonjudgmentally to a child's point of view, calmly communicate their opinions, and leave it to the child to assume responsibility for his own actions.

As nice as it sounds, the democratic family is, was, and always will be fiction. You can, if it makes you feel better, *pretend* to have a democratic family, but pretense is as far as it ever will go. The illusion of democracy in a so-called democratic family is created and maintained with lots of words, lots of discussions, explanations, and lots of asking the children for their opinions. But if you sift down through the rhetoric and finally get to the bottom of things, you will discover an incontrovertible truth: In this so-called democratic family, *someone* always has the final say. That simple fact strips away any and all illusions of democracy. Furthermore, that someone better be an adult, or everyone in the family is in trouble.

In the real world, there is no possibility of a truly democratic relationship between parents and children. Not, at least, as long as the children live at home and rely on parents for emotional, social, and economic protections. Until a child leaves home, there can only be exercises in democracy, and these exercises must be carefully orchestrated by the child's parents, lest they get out of control.

If we're going to draw analogies between families and political systems, then the most ideal form of family government— the one that works best for both parents *and* children—is a "benevolent dictatorship."

In 1976, when I first began using that term, the reaction I often received indicated that people were only hearing the word "dictator." Consequently, they thought I was giving parents permission to be rigidly, even punitively, authoritarian. Well I wasn't, and I'm not.

A benevolent dictatorship is a form of family government in which parents act on the recognition that their most fundamental obligation is to provide a balance of love (benevolence) and authority (dictation) to their children. This is *not* tyranny. Benevolent dictators are *authoritative*, not authoritarian. They do not demand unquestioning obedience. Quite the contrary, they encourage discussion (as opposed to argument), but they make the final decisions. They create rules which are fair and enforce them firmly, but gently. Benevolent dictators don't derive sadistic pleasure out of bossing children around. They govern because they must. They recognize that it's a child's right to be governed well, and every parent's responsibility to provide good government. Beyond all else, they prepare their children for the time when they must govern themselves and *their* children.

In a benevolent dictatorship, as the children grow, they experience increasing responsibility and privilege. This insures that by the time they reach their late teens or early twenties, they are ready for self-government. Having experienced the model in their lives, they know how it works. Within the framework of discipline created for them by benevolently dictatorial parents, children learn the value of independence. They learn it is not something to be taken for granted, but something to be worked for, and therefore, something worth taking care of.

There is a widespread tendency to regard love as a positive force, and authority or discipline as a negative, potentially destructive one. This notion that love is somehow more valuable to a child's upbringing than discipline is what I term "The Great Misunderstanding." The facts are: First, you cannot effectively communicate your love to a child unless you are also a source of effective authority. Second, you cannot effectively discipline unless you are also a source of genuine love.

Authority strengthens parental love. Without that strengthening agent, love becomes indulgent and possessive (overly protective). Likewise, without the tempering effect of love, parental authority becomes overbearing. Love provides meaning and a sense of belonging to a child. Love gives a child reason to strive. Authority provides direction to the child's strivings. Love and authority are not opposite poles, but two sides of the same coin. To be authoritatively loving and lovingly authoritative, *that's* the balancing act parents must master. Achieving that balance is not only essential to a child's security and self-esteem, it's also the key to a parent's sense of self-confidence. *That's* what being a benevolent dictator is all about.

Respect: A Two-Way Street

In the sixties and seventies, these same experts led parents to believe that obedient children were "robots" whose personalities and self-esteem had been squelched by parental heavy-handedness. That simply isn't so. While it's true that parents can intimidate a child into cooperating, that child is also likely to look for opportunities to disobey whenever he thinks he stands a good chance of not getting caught. Fear does not teach obedience. It teaches a child to be cunning.

On the other hand, truly obedient children—that is, children who have invested great amounts of security and, therefore, respect in their parents' authority—are also the world's happiest, most outgoing, and creative kids. It's interesting and most unfortunate that these parenting experts overlooked this connection and dealt in rhetoric, rather than reality. It's unfortunate for millions of American parents who were seduced into subscribing to their nonsensical philosophy that these authors failed to see the connection between parental authority and a child's self-esteem. It's even more unfortunate for the millions of directionless children who were the real victims of this "oversight."

These experts made a big deal of the need for parents to respect children, pointing out that respect is a two-way street. With that, I wholeheartedly agree. But be not deceived! Children show respect for parents by obeying them. Parents show respect for children by expecting them to obey.

Parent Power!

A child needs to become convinced at an early age that there are virtually no limits to his parents' capabilities. The young child's sense of security rests upon the belief that his parents are capable of protecting him, providing for him, and preserving him under any and all circumstances. This requires that parents convey to their children an unquestionable sense of personal power—of *Parent Power*, to borrow the title of my first book. Developmental psychologists have long recognized that young children believe, or want to believe, in their parents' infallibility. This belief is called the "Omnipotency Myth."

An infant's view of the world is egocentric, or self-centered.

He believes that all things exist for him and because of him. His parents exist because he is hungry or uncomfortable or wants to be held. For the first eighteen months or so of the baby's life, parents cooperate with this upside-down conception of how the world works. They cooperate because they must. When the baby is hungry, they feed him because he can't feed himself. When his diaper is messy, they change him because he can't change himself. When he's tired, they soothe him to sleep. When he cries to be held, they hold him. Under the circumstances, it's no wonder that the young child believes his parents were put here to serve him.

Sometime during the child's second year of life, however, parents begin the socialization process. They begin establishing limits and saying "no!" to certain demands. This turnabout contradicts the child's egocentric view of how the world works. His sense of security thus threatened, he struggles to keep things the way they were. This is the essence of the so-called "Terrible Twos." That period from eighteen- to thirty-six months is the single most misunderstood and maligned stage of human development. To be sure, it's a stressful, frustrating, and sometimes even confusing time in the parent/child relationship. But the conflict between parent and child that characterizes this stage is not only unavoidable, but absolutely necessary.

The paradox is this: In order for the young child to develop an enduring, stable sense of security, his parents must first make him temporarily *insecure*. They do this by firmly, but gently, dismantling his egocentric viewpoint and building, in its place, one based on the premise that *they* run the show. If they are successful in replacing egocentricity with parent-centricity, the child develops a respect for them that goes beyond what they are truly capable of. In his eyes, they become *omnipotent*. This perception reflects the child's *need* to see his parents as all-knowing, all-capable people. It follows that parents have a responsibility to present themselves to their children in precisely that light. The idea is not to make the child subservient, but to create for him a nonthreatening authority upon which he can rely.

Parent-centricity, which is the young child's feeling that parents are controlling a world he cannot control for himself, forms the foundation of a new, more functional sense of security. Upon this solid foundation, the child can begin building creative competency in three realms—intellectual, social, and emotional. The establishment of parent-centricity frees the child to go about the business of growing up without always having to worry about what unpredictable thing is going to happen next. This is why consistency is so important in discipline.

Consistency

Consistency is an integral part of expecting children to obey. Consistency makes it possible for a child to predict the consequences of his or her behavior. The ability to anticipate consequences and adjust behavior accordingly is essential to the development of self-discipline, which is the ultimate goal of parental discipline. Without consistency, therefore, discipline isn't discipline. It's confusion.

Discipline is more than just an occasional act. It's a *theme* that should run through every aspect of the parent-child relationship. To be an effective disciplinarian, you must be a model of *self-discipline*. Consistency is the standard against which that self-discipline is measured. The inconsistent parent is, in effect, undisciplined. This parent's attempts at discipline are like the blind trying to lead the blind.

Parents create rules and children test them. Testing is, after all, a child's only way of discovering whether, in fact, a rule truly exists. Telling a child, "This is a rule," isn't convincing enough. Children are concrete thinkers. They must be *shown*.

So, when a child breaks a rule, parents have an obligation to impose some form of discipline. This gets the child's attention and says, "See, we were telling you the truth." Consistency, therefore, is a demonstration of reliability. The more a child feels he can rely on (believe in) his parents, the more secure the child feels. If, however, the child breaks a stated rule and instead of enforcing, parents threaten or talk themselves blue in the face or get excited but don't do anything, the child is forced to test the rule again, and again, and again. Testing of this sort "spins a child's wheels." It wastes time and energy that the child could otherwise be spending in creative, constructive, growth-producing activities. Because consistency frees children from the burden of having to repeatedly test rules, it helps children become all they are capable of becoming.

A child who can predict consequences is in the "driver's seat" of his own discipline. He knows what's going to happen if he does this or that, so he quickly learns to maneuver himself through "traffic." Inconsistency is like a traffic signal that switches unpredictably from red to green, from "right turn" to "left turn," and so on. Inconsistency causes children to have disciplinary "accidents." Consistency, on the other hand, helps them learn to take responsible control of their own lives.

Self-discipline, security, capability, responsibility. They add up to self-esteem. *That's* why consistency is so important.

Children whose parents are inconsistent live in a world of constantly shifting limits, and these children must test their parents just as constantly. This constant testing is what we call "disobedience." If parents' actions are inconsistent with their words, a child learns that they are unreliable and incapable of controlling the world for him. So, in an attempt to reduce his insecurity, the child attempts to control the world on his own. In the process, he becomes self-conscious (and therefore, self-centered), demanding, disrespectful, disruptive, and so on. This quickly becomes a vicious cycle from which a child cannot escape on his own. The more inconsistent his parents are toward his misbehavior, the more they demonstrate their inability to control him. In turn, he becomes even more insecure, and his behavior becomes increasingly agitated and inappropriate. As his behavior worsens, so does his parents' inconsistency. And 'round and 'round they will go, until that child's parents learn the art of benevolent dictation. When previously inconsistent parents finally take control away from a misbehaving child, that child experiences a immense sense of relief and security. But the trick to never having to wrestle control away from a misbehaving child is to truly *expect* obedience in the first place.

To illustrate the importance of consistency, consider the job of basketball referee: The referee's job is simply to enforce the rules, consistently and dispassionately. Imagine the chaos that would result if nearly every time a rule was broken, he complained, threatened, gave second chances and, every so often, vented his self-imposed frustrations by launching into a red-faced emotional tirade. Let's join just such a game in progress:

A player on the Red Team takes a pass from one of his teammates and drives toward the basket for a lay-up. As he nears the goal, a Blue player sticks out a foot and sends the Red player sprawling unceremoniously across the floor. Immediately, the referee blows his whistle. As play stops, he points an accusing finger at the offender.

"Was that an accident, or did you trip him on purpose?" the referee demands. Looking sheepish, the Blue player answers, "It was just an accident, honest. I didn't mean to."

"Well, okay," the referee says, "I'll let it go this time, but don't let it happen again."

The next incident occurs as a Blue player sets up to take a shot from the corner. Before he can release the ball, a Red player leaps up from behind and grabs his arm, preventing the shot. Again, the referee blows his whistle, stops play, and confronts the guilty player.

"How many times have I told you not to do that?" he asks, exasperated. "You let me tell you something! I'm about to run out of patience with you! The next time you do something like that, you'll be sorry, believe me!"

Soon, another infraction occurs, and another confrontation: "Why did you *do* that?" the referee pleads.

The player shrugs his shoulders and looks down at the floor. "I don't know," he replies.

"What, in God's name, am I going to do with you?" the referee shrieks, holding his head in his hands.

As the clock ticks on, fouls become more frequent and obvious. With nearly every one, the referee's reaction is the same—reprimand, threat, complaint, etc. Occasionally, he actually follows through with a penalty, but only after putting on a great display of verbal and physical histrionics.

Eventually, the game is in shambles, a virtual free-for-all. Players push, trip, and even hit one another for control of the ball. All the while, the referee runs around red-faced and sweating, looking increasingly distraught. Finally, as the melee reaches peak intensity, he suddenly twists his body in ten different directions at once, shouts, "I've had it!" and looks pleadingly toward the heavens. We leave the referee there, petitioning the powers that be for relief from his terrible burden.

This description may sound familiar, since it typifies the disciplinary "tone" of many an American family. Children test rules, and parents threaten, berate, plead, and complain, all the while becoming increasingly frustrated. Finally, they meltdown in a spasm of exasperation. For a while, all's quiet. Then, slowly, the children come out of "hiding" and once again, the snowball begins its downhill descent.

Inconsistency causes children to "play" at misbehavior in much the same way compulsive gamblers play at games of chance. Compulsive gamblers keep gambling, even when they're losing their shirts, precisely because they can never predict when they're going to win. This randomness fuels the perpetual fantasy that Lady Luck might be just one more throw of the dice away. In the same manner, unpredictable discipline causes children to keep throwing the dice of misbehavior. The only difference between compulsive gamblers and children is that while gamblers eventually run out of money, children never run out of energy!

Parents who truly *expect* obedience from children discipline consistently and dispassionately. Consequently, discipline never becomes a "Big Deal," something parents find themselves constantly stumbling over. A matter-of-fact attitude toward discipline creates a calm, relaxed atmosphere in which everyone's "place" is clear. This allows life within a family to be simple, as it should be.

Communication

Expecting children to obey has a lot to do with how parents communicate instructions to children. As I pointed out earlier, many, if not most, parents communicate instructions in a wishful, wishy-washy manner. They plead, bargain, argue, threaten, and then—when they've finally reached the end of their ropes—they lower the boom. This sort of disciplinary style creates and perpetuates an atmosphere of uncertainty and tension within the parent-child relationship.

When giving instructions to children, parents should be commanding, concise, and concrete. These are the "Three C's of Good Communication."

BE COMMANDING: Speak directly to the child and preface instructions with authoritative statements, such as "I want you to . . ." or "It's time for you to . . ." or "You need to. . . ." In other words, don't beat around the bush. If you want a child to do something, you must tell him in no uncertain terms. The more uncertain your terms, the more uncertain the outcome.

BE CONCISE: Don't use fifty words when five will do. Almost all of us were lectured as children, and we all remember hating it. We know from that experience that as soon as the lecturer gets going, a fuse blows somewhere between the child's ears and brain.

BE CONCRETE: Speak in terms that are down-to-earth, rather than abstract. Use language that refers to the specific *behavior* you expect, as opposed to the *attitude*. "I want you to be *good* in church this morning" is vague, abstract. "While we're in church, I want you to sit quietly next to me" is clear and concrete. When parents leave doubt in a child's mind as to just exactly what they expect, the child can be counted on to give himself the benefit of that doubt.

Some of the more common errors of communication parents commit include:

—*Phrasing instructions as if they were questions.* This implies choice, when no choice actually exists.
Wrong: "How about picking up these toys so we can start getting ready for bed?"
Right: "It's almost time for bed. You need to pick up your toys and put them away."

—*Phrasing expectations in abstract, rather than concrete, terms.* Using words like "good," "responsible," and "nice" leaves the parent's actual meaning open to interpretation.
Wrong: "I want you to be *good* while we're in the store."
Right: "While we're in the store, I want you to walk next to me and ask permission before touching anything."

56

—*Stringing instructions together.* The mind of a child younger than five has difficulty "holding" more than one instruction at a time. With children older than five, but younger than twelve, it's best to give no more than two instructions at a time. If it's not convenient to hand out chores in this patient fashion, then give the child a list. If he or she isn't yet literate, use drawings.

Wrong: "Today, I want you to clean your room, take out the garbage, feed the dog, pick up the toys in the den, and help me move these boxes into the attic."

Right: "The first thing I want you to do today is clean your room. When you finish, let me know, and I'll tell you what comes next."

—*Preceding instructions with, "Let's . . ."* This is another passive, nonauthoritative form of communication. When you expect a child to do a chore on his or her own, say so. Don't confuse the issue and open the door for resistance by implying that you're willing to pitch in.

Wrong: "Let's set the table, okay?"

Right: "It's time for you to set the table."

—*Following instructions with reasons or explanations.* Putting the reason last attracts the child's attention to *it*, rather than the instruction itself. This makes argument more likely.

Wrong: "It's time to get off the swing so we can go home."

Right: "It's time for us to go home now. Get off the swing and come with me."

—*Making an instruction into a "sales pitch."* This might work with small children, but by the time a child is four or five, he's wise to ploys of this sort, and the chance of non-compliance increases.

Wrong: "Hey, Sissy! Guess what? Mom's cooked a really great supper tonight! Let's say goodbye to Cindy and go see Mom's surprise!"

Right: "It's time for supper, Sissy. You need to say goodbye to Cindy and come inside."

—*Giving instructions with an open-ended time frame.*

Wrong: "Billy, I need you to mow the lawn some time today, when you get a chance."

Right: "Billy, I want you to mow the lawn today, and I want you to be finished by the time I get home at six o'clock."

—*Expressing instructions in the form of wishes.* This amounts to nothing more than passive complaint about the child's behavior. Children don't grant wishes, genies do.
Wrong: "I wish you'd stop chewing with your mouth open."
Right: "Stop chewing with your mouth open."

Have a Plan!

Expecting children to obey also involves having a plan for what you are going to do if they don't. In fact, the secret to virtually frustration-free discipline is, first, have a plan; then, carry it through consistently.

Most parents discipline by the seat of their pants. Consequently, when misbehavior occurs, they respond emotionally, rather than commonsensically. If businesses were run in this absurd manner, they would all be bankrupt in no time. To make a profit, a business must operate according to a plan. Its managers must anticipate potential problems and develop strategies for dealing with them, if and when they occur. The same goes for parents who value effective discipline. They, too, must anticipate problems and be ready to deal authoritatively with them. I call this "Striking While the Iron is Cold." This simply means that the most effective time for dealing with misbehavior is *before* it occurs. Striking while the iron is cold is a three-step process:

—*Anticipate*: Anticipate the problem, based either on a knowledge of the child or of children in general.

—*Plan*: Develop a strategy for dealing with the problem.

—*Communicate*: Talk with the child about the problem, defining it and letting the child in on the strategy (but not asking permission to use it!).

By striking while the iron is cold, you put yourself in the most effective position possible for striking when the iron gets hot. When the heat is on, implement your strategy, following through as promised, and continue to follow through, as needed, until the problem is solved.

In the language of the business world, striking while the iron is cold is *pro-active*, as opposed to *reactive*. In parenting, as in business, to deal with problems pro-actively is to control them, as opposed to letting them control you.

Let's see how this strategic process can be applied to a typical behavior problem. Take Rodney, a five-year-old, who persists in getting out of bed to ask unnecessary questions and make inappropriate requests. To make him stay in bed, Rodney's parents have threatened, bribed, spanked, and screamed—all examples of ineffective, knee-jerk (reactive) emotional responses.

Finally, Rodney's parents wisely decide to strike while the iron is cold. They have no trouble anticipating the problem, since it's happened every night for the past two years, so they go straight to the planning stage. They decide Rodney will be allowed out of bed one time, and one time only, to ask a question or make a request. When they tuck him in, they'll give him a "ticket," consisting simply of a small rectangle of colored construction paper. Rodney can use this one ticket to "purchase" the privilege of getting out of bed.

When he gets out of bed, as he surely will, he hands his parents the ticket. In return, they let him ask a question or tell them something. Then, they put him back to bed. If, for whatever reason (including "needing" to go to the bathroom), he gets up again, his parents keep him indoors the next day and put him to bed one hour early (with a ticket).

Having made their plans, his parents calmly communicate their decision to Rodney at five o'clock one afternoon. As they're preparing him for bed, they remind him of the "new deal." Then they tuck him in, give him his ticket, and turn out the lights.

Does Rodney get out of bed? Of course! Does he get out of bed more than once? Of course! You see, Rodney must test the rule in order to find out if it really exists.

The next day, Rodney's parents deliver his punishment as promised. That night, he gets out of bed twice. The next day, his parents again keep him indoors and put him to bed early. The third night, Rodney gets out of bed ten times. He's trying to find out if his parents will stick to the plan if he acts oblivious to it. The next day, his parents stick to the plan. That night, Rodney gets out of bed one time, and no more. Over the next few weeks, Rodney tests on several more occasions. Each time, he finds out that his parents are still sticking to the plan. At last, Rodney stops testing. In fact, he eventually stops getting out of bed altogether! And Rodney sleeps easier, knowing his parents mean what they say.

As this example points out, good discipline doesn't have to be complicated. Rather, it must be well organized, easily communicated, and easily dispensed. The simpler, the better!

Keep Things Simple!

Nothing will kill a discipline plan quicker than weighing it down with dozens of unnecessary "if, then" considerations. Example: "If you clean your room, you get a star. If you don't, you get a check. At the end of the week, we subtract checks from stars, and that determines your allowance. If there are more checks than stars, however, you owe us money, which we take off the top of *next week's* allowance. If there are no checks, you get a bonus. If, however, you owe us more than the bonus, the bonus is applied to the debt." See what I mean? Einstein couldn't have kept all that straight.

Another way of dooming discipline to failure is to bite off more than you can chew. Let's take, for example, a child who is destructive, disobedient, irresponsible, unmotivated, aggressive, disrespectful, bossy, and loud. Instead of tackling all the problems at once, which would be like wrestling with an octopus, you would do better to concentrate your energies on just one of them. Solving one problem puts you in good position to solve another, and then another, and so on.

The parents of two children, ages five and two, were having the usual problems that come with children of those ages. You know, they sassed, squabbled, screamed, jumped on furniture, wrote on walls, got into everything, and created general bedlam. These parents spent lots of time and energy racing from one child to another, one thing to the next, driving themselves bananas in the process. They reminded me of the plate-spinners that used to appear on "The Ed Sullivan Show." The more these parents tried to accomplish, the less they accomplished. "Pick three problems," I told them.

They picked sassing, squabbling, and screaming. Neither child could read, so we drew a picture for each problem. Screaming was represented by a stick-child with mouth wide open; squabbling by two stick-children with mouths wide open; sassing by one stick-child sticking stick-tongue out at stick-parent. Artists, we weren't.

The pictures were posted on the refrigerator, and the children were told what each of them meant. The parents bought a timer and kept it handy to the children's rooms. When one of the targeted behaviors occurred, the parent closest to the scene would identify the behavior (i.e., "That's sassing"), and say, "That's on one of your pictures and means you have to go to your room(s)." A squabble sent both children to their respective rooms, regardless of who "started" it.

The parent would take the offending child or children to his/her/their room(s), set the timer for ten minutes, and walk away. When the bell rang, the kids could come out of their neutral corners.

Talking with these parents, I stressed the importance of adhering to what I call "The Referee's Rule": No threats, second chances, or deals.

"When you see an infraction," I said, speaking figuratively, "blow the whistle and assess the penalty. Remember that in hesitation or indecision, all is lost!"

I saw them again three weeks later. The mother started off by telling me she finally found a whistle at a sporting goods store.

"Wait a minute," I said. "You mean you actually went out and bought a real whistle?"

"Sure did!" she said. "It sounded like a good idea to me. When we're at home, I wear it around my neck. When I blow the whistle, the kids march to their rooms. I don't even have to tell them to go. Better yet, they set the timer themselves."

I asked how she felt about the plan, and here's what she told me, word-for-word: "I feel more confident in my parenting skills and more in control of the kids. Furthermore, the kids are reacting in a way that tells me *they're* more confident of my authority. They've learned my limits. Before, it seemed we were always in a frenzy. Now, the household is calm. It's a very organized feeling, and everyone is happier."

Strike another blow for simplicity.

Negotiating from a Position of Power

Because I often speak and write about the power of "Because I said so," I am frequently asked whether Willie and I ever gave Eric and Amy reasons or permitted discussion of rules and such. On both counts, the answer is, "Yes, we did." We *always* gave our children, now ages twenty and sixteen, reasons for our decisions. One of those reasons was "Because I said so" or a variation on that theme. We gave other reasons only when they were more honest than "Because I said so," which is, as I've already said, the most honest answer more often than not.

When we gave reasons other than "Because I said so," we never expected the children to agree, and they never disappointed us. Nor did we try to persuade them to our point of view. After all, our points of view have been more than forty years in the making. We're not foolish enough to think we can rush Mother Nature! As Orson Welles once said, "No mind before its time." Or was that Groucho Marx?

Whereas we refused to waste time, ours and theirs, by getting into arguments with them, we taught them how to get their way. A typical exchange went something like this:

A much-younger Eric comes to me with a request, to which I say, "No." He becomes visibly agitated, throws arms out to his sides, strains forward, and asks, "Why not!?" in a voice that sounds like fingernails being dragged across a chalkboard.

"Wrong, Eric," I say. "That's *not* the way to do it. If you want me to give you an explanation, you must ask for it properly. By that I mean you must compose yourself and ask in a manner that's not irritating. So try again, from the top."

He stands for a moment, looking slightly disgusted, then makes his request a second time. Again, I say, "No." He takes a deep breath and says, "Would you mind telling me why?"

"Good job," I say. "No, Eric, I don't mind telling you why."

With that, I begin explaining myself. Before I finish my first sentence, however, Eric interrupts with, "But, Dad!"

"No, Eric," I say, "you've blown it again! When you ask someone for an explanation, you have an obligation to listen, whether you agree or not. After I give my reason, it's your turn to tell me why you disagree. Got that?"

Eric nods, with a heavy sigh.

"Good! Let's take it from the top again."

"Aw, Dad!" he complains, "You've got to be kidding."

"No, I'm not kidding. We're going to stand here together until you get the whole thing right. Unless, that is, you want to stop right here. In that case, you're going to have to live with my original answer. What'll it be?"

Begrudgingly, he starts over. Eventually, after much trial and error, he finally gets it right. When he does, I reward his efforts by meeting him halfway. This teaches him to negotiate, rather than argue and complain, for what he wants.

Some people might say this sounds like a lot of trouble, but it really isn't. Especially not when you consider the pay-off. Besides, it was my responsibility to teach Eric the skills he needed to live a successful life.

What I did with Eric was no different than what a supervisor does when teaching an employee a new job. The supervisor teaches the task one step at a time. If the employee makes a mistake at some point in the sequence, the supervisor corrects it and has the employee start over from the top. In that manner, the employee eventually learns the entire sequence.

As I said, it was my responsibility to teach Eric the art of negotiation; it was Eric's responsibility to use it to his advantage. And use it he did, to create more freedom for himself during his high school years than most youngsters enjoy until they're in college.

And it all traced back to "Because I said so."

Decision-Making

Decisions, decisions. Raising a child certainly involves its share. From the moment of birth through eighteen or more years of gradual emancipation, decisions never stop demanding a parent's time. No sooner have you made one than you must make another, and then another, and so on.

To complicate matters, there are not only those decisions *you* have to make, but also the decisions you must help your child make—what to wear to school, whom to invite over to spend the night, how to handle conflicts with other children, etc.

It's enough to drive a parent nuts and, indeed, we all veer off in that direction every once in a while. Most of us return from these little side trips with only minor scars, but some of us become lost forever. Some parents drive themselves to distraction simply because they get hung up in details. To them, every decision seems momentous, from whether to have the child brush his teeth before or after breakfast to whether he should or shouldn't be retained in the third grade. Believing that any wrong decision has the potential of ruining the child's future, these parents become obsessed with always making "right" ones.

This raises an interesting question: "What is a *right* decision?"

Many parents mistakenly think that for any given childrearing situation, there is but one *correct* course of action. That's like believing that of the forty or so items on a restaurant menu, there's just *one* perfectly suited to your taste. The fact is, the *way* in which parents make decisions is far more important than the content of the decisions themselves. The same applies to managing a business.

An effective manager is decisive. He doesn't waste time and energy obsessing over details. He trusts his intuition and common sense. More than anything else, a good manager realizes it's less important to always be "right" than to always inspire confidence and a sense of purpose in those he manages. He knows that wrong decisions are less harmful to an organization than a faulty decision-making style. To the degree that a manager is obsessive or indecisive, he promotes distrust, insecurity, and conflict in the workplace. Indecisive parents create similar problems in the home.

Do you see yourself in the following description?

—You dwell on decisions, rather than trusting your feelings and your common sense and just "snapping them off." Obsessing over every decision, large or small, wastes time, invites arguments, and is a sign to the child that he can probably get his way if he pushes hard enough.

—You include your child in too many decisions. Asking a child's opinion about some things has its place, but when that's the rule rather than the exception, the likelihood of conflict between parent and child increases.

—If your child dislikes a decision you've made, you're almost certain to compromise, if not give in. Parents give in to avoid conflict. Unfortunately, the more conflict they avoid, the more they ultimately have to deal with.

—You constantly explain yourself to your child. As I've previously said, children don't really want explanations, they want arguments. Requesting the explanation is nothing more than a means to that end.

If that shoe fits, you need to stop making your life—as well as your child's—so complicated. Start trusting your feelings. Stop worrying that you're going to traumatize your child for life if you make a bad decision. Bad decisions don't do long-term damage. Bad *people* do.

"Wait 'til Your Father Gets Home"

Or so my mother would say whenever my relentlessly obnoxious behavior became too much for her to handle. And it never failed to work. Those six words always brought me back to reality.

"No, Ma, wait, I mean, I'm sorry, really, I didn't mean it, I was wrong and, like I said, I'm, listen, I'll do anything, just please, don't, I mean, don't tell Dad, please, I'll be good, I'm sorry, oh, Ma, you know what he'll do, and you don't want my blood on your hands do you, Ma, huh? Do you?"

But it was no good. She'd tell him anyway. And he would descend upon me and smite me with his wrath. And for a while, I'd hate them both, but I'd be good. For a while.

"Wait 'til your father gets home" was the way many of the homemaker-mothers of my parents' generation controlled their children. And it usually worked, but at no small price, for in the process we learned to fear and sometimes even hate our fathers. We also learned just how far we could push our mothers before they'd crack. And because we were children, and it's a child's nature to flirt with danger, we made a game of dancing dangerously close to the line, then backing off at the last moment. Sometimes we won; sometimes we lost.

But between the lines, inside the fear, other things were learned. Chief among them was the idea that moms/women were weak and ineffectual while dads/men were strong and worthy of respect. Moms yell and threaten; dads take action. In short, we learned that men were more competent than women, and then we started acting as if that were true.

Finally, the women of our generation rebelled, and justly so. Unfortunately, many of them saw the problem in the one-dimensional language of us *versus* them. Where we could and should have been comrades-in-arms, we became opponents. The anger and self-righteousness of the women's movement put men on the defensive. The movement also failed to see that what started in the home had to be resolved in the home before it could be resolved on any larger scale. In short, the cart was put before the horse.

The way a child is disciplined will do much to shape his or her attitudes toward and perceptions of men and women. As much as is possible then, discipline should be handled such that children do not wind up viewing their fathers as "heavies" and their mothers as "pushovers" or vice versa. When Mom is on the front lines, she should handle the discipline. The same goes for Dad. And their discipline should be relatively consistent, not only from situation to situation, but also from parent to parent. That prevents either parent from coming across as stronger/more competent than the other.

But these are *general* rules, and can be violated when circumstances demand. There are times when it's completely appropriate to say, "I'm going to wait until your father/mother gets home. We're going to handle this problem together. Meanwhile, you're going to stay in your room." This is the way to handle the Big Stuff, the stuff that doesn't happen every day. Stuff like a child cursing a teacher or throwing a rock at a passing car.

This sends the child a strong message: "We stand together. This is not a one-person show." The more a child hears that message, the more likely it is he will develop a functional perception of men and women as *partners* instead of opponents. If we would all see to it that each and every child was raised that way, we'd truly be on the road to healing ourselves.

The Pitfalls of Praise

Beware of truisms. Often enough, truisms turn out to be false-isms, and this is particularly the case within the pseudo-science of "parenting."

Most people, for example, think children need a lot of praise, and that praise builds self-esteem. Both are false-isms. The fact-isms are that children need little praise, and that praise can be either constructive or destructive to a child's self-esteem. The turning point is also, as we shall see, the reference point.

Several years ago, a team of researchers divided twenty, five-year-old children into two groups of ten. Each group was taken into a large activity area staffed by several "teachers." In the middle of the room stood a table overflowing with art supplies of every sort—colored paper, clay, crayons, paints, scissors, and so on. After a brief "get acquainted" period, the teachers directed the children to sit down and "make something."

With the first group, the teachers moved around the table giving lots of praise, holding each project up for everyone to see, and generally effervescing with enthusiasm for what the children were doing.

These same teachers were considerably more reserved with children in the second group. Instead of hovering, they stayed back from the table, involved in tasks of their own. Occasionally, one of them would ask if anyone needed help or more supplies. If a child showed his project to a teacher, obviously seeking praise, the teacher would respond with a few warm words.

The next day, the teachers brought the children back to the room. This time, they were allowed one hour of free play. The researchers kept track of the time children in each of the groups spent playing with the art material.

Lo and behold! Children in the first group avoided the art table as if it were contaminated; children in the second spent little time anywhere else. This tells us that too much praise is negative, and causes children to actually avoid the activities, people, and places associated with it.

Psychologists make a distinction between evaluative and descriptive praise. Evaluative praise is judgmental and personal. For instance, when Billy brings his teacher a leaf collection, the teacher exclaims, "Oh, Billy, you're such a hard worker and a joy to teach. If it wasn't for you, this year would have been terribly routine for me."

By implication, evaluative praise takes away the child's right to be imperfect. As a result, the child may begin to internalize an unreasonably high standard of excellence for himself and may eventually begin feeling that he "can't measure up." The end results of evaluative praise are feelings of inadequacy and discouragement, quite the opposite of what was intended.

Descriptive praise has no such built-in dangers. It is, as the name implies, simply a description, an acknowledgment of accomplishment. In the case of Billy and his leaf collection, the teacher could have said, "You obviously put a lot of time and effort into this collection, Billy. Thank you for sharing this with the class."

Like sugar, praise can be habit-forming. Children who are praised either excessively or evaluatively often develop a dependence on outside approval. A child so hooked is like a tire with a slow leak: Every so often, he must be pumped up or he'll go flat.

Sometimes, adults praise things that shouldn't be praised, like using the toilet properly. We need not, should not, praise children for growing up. A simple acknowledgment will suffice, because growth is its own reward. The adult who praises for an act of self-sufficiency is, in effect, appropriating the inherent pleasure of the event—stealing the child's thunder.

Praise can also backfire, particularly in the case of a child with low self-esteem. Praise is inconsistent with this child's self-image, particularly if the praise is evaluative. The mismatch between message and image generates anxiety, which the child may attempt to reduce by misbehaving—setting the record straight.

In other words, praise is not something to be tossed out carelessly. Be conservative and thoughtful about it. Above all else, with praise as with punishment, take aim at the act, *not* the child.

Questions?

Q: My five-year-old son has difficulty making decisions. He starts the day unable to decide what he wants for breakfast. The more things I suggest, the more confused he becomes. During the day, he agonizes over everything from what friend to invite over to what toy to play with. At bedtime, he can't decide what book he wants read to him. Then he can't decide what clothes he wants to wear the following day. Since both my mother and I have problems making decisions, I'm beginning to wonder whether his problem might be genetic. Any ideas?

A: Your son is having problems making decisions because you're giving him too many decisions to make.

A problem doesn't have to be genetic in order for it to get handed down from one generation to the next. Indecisive people try to get other people to make decisions for them. When you were a child, your mother probably dealt with her indecisiveness by asking you to make not only too many decisions, but also decisions you weren't capable of making. In so doing, she overloaded your decision-making capacity, and you eventually became indecisive. Now that you have a child of your own, you're passing that indecisiveness along by asking him to make too many decisions. And 'round and 'round you go, and where you stop . . . nobody can decide.

The solution is obvious. You must stop expecting your son to make so many decisions. But wait! That means *you're* going to have to start making more decisions yourself. We need, therefore, to take a closer look at your own indecisiveness.

Indecisive parents are usually afraid of making mistakes.

They think bad decisions scar children for life, so they end up making no firm decisions at all, which is one of the biggest mistakes a parent can *ever* make. The fact is, 'tis better for a parent to make a mistake every day than to be generally indecisive. Bad decisions can either be shrugged off with an "Oh, well," or corrected. A faulty decision-making style, however, can spell long-term trouble.

A child's sense of security is founded upon parental love and authority. Parents demonstrate the latter by being decisive. Parental indecisiveness causes children to feel insecure. That insecurity is likely to be expressed in the form of behavior problems. So you see? The more you try to avoid making mistakes that could cause problems, the more problems you cause.

So, get decisive! Time's a-wastin'!

Tonight, while you're preparing your son for bed, go stand in front of the bookshelf and, with your eyes closed, pick out a book. Say, "This is the book I'm reading to you tonight." *Don't* say, "Is this one okay?" That's not decisive! If he says the book you picked isn't the one he wants, say, "Well, it's the one I want to read, so lie down and enjoy."

When you finish the book, pick an outfit, any outfit, for him to wear the next day. Say, "Put these on when you wake up." Don't ask if he approves, and if he questions your selection, say, "Because it's what I've decided." Then tuck him in and say goodnight.

The next morning, when he gets up, blow his young mind by fixing a breakfast and putting it in front of him with, "Here's your breakfast." If he says it's not what he wants, tell him he doesn't have to eat it. Then go sit down and read the paper. You see how simple this is?

Anytime you see him becoming indecisive, either walk away (if you have the time) or take over (if you don't). If you show him how decisions are made, it shouldn't be long before he begins following your lead and taking better control of his own life.

Q: Our son, Ernie, recently decided to become a truly "Terrible" two-year-old. My husband thinks Ernie is old enough to be spanked, but I'm not so sure. What do you think?

A: That depends on your definition of spankings, as well as when and how you plan to use them. In my view, a spanking is a spanking only if the following conditions are adhered to:
—The parent administers it with his or her hand only.
—The parent's hand makes contact with the child's rear end only.
—The hand strikes the rear no more than three times.

Anything else is a beating. I also recommend that if parents are going to spank, they do so as a *first* resort. The more parents threaten, the more frustration they build, and the more likely it is they will spank in a rage.

Contrary to accepted wisdom, parents should *always* spank in anger. If the parent isn't angry, then a spanking isn't justified. A first-resort spanking delivered in anger is over quickly. The child isn't likely to feel resentment, and the parent isn't likely to feel guilt.

Some people think spankings of any sort constitute child abuse. I don't. Some parents *do* spank abusively, but then any form of discipline, even talking to a child, can be delivered destructively.

Other people think that spankings are the most effective form of discipline there is. I don't agree with that either. In and of themselves, spankings do not motivate appropriate behavior. A spanking accompanied by a period of restriction or a brief reprimand will have a much greater positive effect than a spanking alone. Furthermore, children who receive a lot of spankings often become "immune" to them. The less parents spank, therefore, the more effective each spanking will be.

A spanking is really nothing more than a form of nonverbal communication. It's an exclamation point of sorts, placed in *front* of a verbal message. It says, "Now hear this!" A spanking serves as a reminder of authority and a demonstration of disapproval. But it's no substitute for more effective forms of discipline, verbal or otherwise.

There are some who use Biblical references to the "rod" to justify using spankings as a primary, and frequent, form of discipline. I would simply point out that the "rod" was a symbol of authority in ancient times. Those passages, therefore, are more accurately interpreted to mean that parents who spare their authority will certainly spoil their children.

As a rule, spankings are not effective with two-year-olds. In the first place, twos are decidedly determined little people, and spankings often provoke even greater determination. Furthermore, this-age child quickly forgets a spanking. Two minutes later, he's back doing the same thing. A firm but gentle approach to discipline, involving lots of "Grandma's Rule"—the child can do or have what he wants when he's done what his parents want—is much more effective than spankings.

Q: Our five-year-old daughter, Margo, demands attention constantly. If we're in public, she asks for everything that catches her fancy and cries if we say "no." At home, if we have guests, she interrupts conversations and is loud and sassy. When one of us tells her to do something, she ignores us. If we press the point, she either cries or complains or becomes downright defiant. Nearly every request, even a simple one, turns into a confrontation. In every other respect, she is delightful. How can we control her without repressing her personality?

A: I have an idea, and I guarantee it will not harm Margo's personality. First, make a list of the behaviors you want your daughter to eliminate, starting with problems that take place at home. For example, the list might read:

1. When we tell Margo to do something (or stop doing something), she (a) pretends not to hear us, (b) cries, (c) complains, (d) says, "I won't!"
2. When we have company, Margo is loud.
3. Margo interrupts people when they are talking.
4. When Margo doesn't get her way, she cries.

Next, buy a portable kitchen timer and select an isolated place in your house where Margo can sit for five minutes at a time.

With everything in place, sit down and explain the program to Margo. Go over the problem behavior list with her, giving examples to make the descriptions clear.

"Margo, these are things we want you to stop doing. In the past, we have ranted and raved and gone blue in the face when you did these things. We are putting this list on the refrigerator. When you do something on it, we are going to take you to the downstairs bathroom and set this timer for five minutes. When the bell rings, you can come out."

To make this work, you must not make threats or give second chances. In other words, if Margo displays one of the behaviors on the problem behavior list, don't threaten her with the bathroom. Just put her there, set the timer, and walk away. Upon telling Margo she's headed for the bathroom, she may suddenly decide to cooperate and say, "I'll be good!" or words to that effect. If so, just say, "You can be good when you come out of the bathroom," and follow through with the plan.

It may only take a week or so before you see change in Margo's behavior, but it will take at least three to six months of following through before good habits completely replace the bad ones.

Q: Our eight-year-old son is a "forgetter." He can't seem to remember anything we tell him. Assign him a chore; he forgets. Give him a message for someone; it never gets there. If we tell him to do two things, one gets done. Maybe. As he gets older, he seems to be getting worse. What, if anything, can we do to help improve his memory?

A: Take heart! After being lost for nearly a generation, the secret to improving your son's memory has been found and, lucky for you, it works just as well as ever. Not only that, but it doesn't cost a penny and comes with a guarantee of satisfaction. It's called discipline.

You can call your son "forgetful" if it makes you feel better. I'd call him disobedient. "I forgot" is an evasive way of saying, "I didn't want to" or something equally noncompliant.

Consider the fact that "forgetting" is always so suspiciously selective. The same child who almost always "forgets" to feed the dogs or come in when the streetlights go on, never forgets things like ice cream in the refrigerator or the casual mention his parents made, several weeks ago, of a possible trip to the zoo. I'll just bet your son remembers things he wants to remember and "forgets" those things he would rather do without, like chores.

To improve his memory, first make a list of his privileges, like so:

RIDE YOUR BIKE
GO OUTSIDE
HAVE A FRIEND OVER
WATCH TELEVISION

Put the list on the refrigerator and every time he "forgets" something, cross off the highest remaining privilege, starting with RIDE YOUR BIKE. Every privilege crossed off is lost until the following Monday. After you've tucked your son into bed on Sunday, wipe the slate clean by taking the old list down and posting a new one.

By taxing his so-called forgetfulness in this painless manner, you make him responsible for the problem. If you're consistent, then I can virtually guarantee that over the next few months, you'll see an amazing improvement in his memory!

Q: We have two sons, ages nine and seven. Except for an occasional spat, they get along just fine. Too fine, in fact. Whenever we discipline one of them, the other jumps in to tell us we're not being fair. They've occasionally flustered us into backing down altogether. We've talked ourselves blue in the face, but to no avail. What can we say to keep them from interfering in one another's discipline?

A: You needn't do any more talking than you've already done. If talking is going to solve a problem, parents won't have to talk more than once, maybe twice. Your boys aren't stupid. They both know you don't want them interfering in your discipline. As it stands, you've said all you possibly can say on the subject. In fact, you've probably repeated yourself time and time again. More talking will only bring the same results: None.

Your problem isn't that you haven't made yourself clear. It's that you've failed to convince the boys you mean business. Up until now, you've given them every reason to believe you don't mean what you say. You said it yourself: When one of them interferes, you might back down. And as you've discovered, you don't have to back down often to keep the problem alive.

Like a compulsive gambler throwing quarters into a slot machine, children don't have to be rewarded often for misbehavior to keep on misbehaving. If you punish a certain misbehavior forty-nine times and reward it once, that one reward is more powerful and motivating than the forty-nine previous punishments.

Here's how to cure your boys from "gambling": The next time you begin disciplining one of them and the other complains that you're not being fair, say, "Come to think of it, you're right. Fair means treating both of you the same. Therefore, since you decided to interfere, you'll receive the same punishment as your brother."

In this case, don't spoil your fun by warning them in advance that this is what you're going to do. Surprise them with your fairness! That should give them something to think about!

Q: Our eight-year-old son has recently started lying to us. For example, when we questioned him about a bathroom drain that had become mysteriously plugged with bubble gum, he swore he had nothing to do with it. After giving him the "third degree," he finally admitted to it but was unable to tell us why he had lied. That's just one of several times we've caught him lying in the past few weeks. We've let him know that his punishment will always be worse if he lies, but that hasn't proven to be an effective deterrent. What does this mean and what should we do about it?

A: It means he's a typical eight-year-old who, like most other children his age or thereabouts, is trying his hand at various forms of relatively harmless mischief, including the mischief of trying everything he can think of to throw the bloodhounds off his trail when he's done something wrong.

Why now? Good question. Up until age eight or nine, children tend to hold their parents in great awe. They think we big people are capable of just about anything; that we can read minds, see through walls, and stuff like that. This perception of parents as powerful and all-knowing is, in fact, fairly essential to the young child's sense of security.

As the single-digit years draw to a close, however, children begin to realize we aren't quite as smart as they thought. They begin trying to expose the full extent of our stupidity by mis-behaving and then playing innocent when confronted with the circumstantial evidence of their guilt.

When these things began happening with our children, Willie and I applied the "Ask them no questions, they'll tell you no lies" rule. If, for instance, I was fairly certain that Number-One-Son had put a hole in the wall, I might say, "Eric, for putting a hole in the wall, we're going to behead you in the morning. Do you have any last wishes?"

In other words, instead of asking the foolish question, I would make a statement. More often than not, the statement would include a consequence. Statements are assertive. As such, they are highly effective at preventing games of cat-and-mouse.

"Did you do this?" questions, because they are passive in nature, invite denial. And once the chase is on, the child is squarely in control of how long the chase lasts. This introduces a second, highly reinforcing element into the scenario—namely, power.

So, going back to your question, you made your first mis-take when you asked your son, "Did you put bubble gum in the drain?" You could have saved lots of time and energy by saying something like, "You're going to live in the bathroom until you figure out a way of getting the bubble gum out of the drain."

If he had protested his innocence, you could have simply said, "This isn't a court of law. It's a family and we're not going to waste everyone's time with a trial. I've made a decision and you're going to do as you're told."

Sure, you might be wrong, but in all likelihood you're right. As a parent, I found that my first intuitions about who-done-it were correct at least 90 percent of the time. The way I figure it, being wrong 10 percent of the time was less harmful to my children than giving them opportunity after opportunity to practice pulling the wool over people's eyes.

Q: What do you think the role of grandparents should be in the raising of children? Should grandparents be expected to always support the parents' rules and methods of enforcement?

A: I agree with late anthropologist Margaret Mead who once wrote, "Grandparents need grandchildren to keep the changing world alive for them, and grandchildren need grandparents to help them know who they are and to give them a sense of human experience in a (past) world they cannot know."

Grandparents can and should be one of a child's most valuable resources. At their best, grandparents are gentle teachers of the way life was, and perhaps the way it always should be. Grandparents can also be among parents' most valuable resources, demonstrating patience and tempering the often brittle seriousness of parenting with the flexibility and humor that only an appreciation for the full panorama of human life can bring.

Problems can arise when grandparents continue to perceive and treat their offspring as children long after their maturity and emancipation. In those cases, the grandchildren often become trapped in the middle of a power struggle between grandparents and parents. No one can win contests such as these, but the biggest losers are always the children.

When Eric was born, Willie and I, like many young parents, tended to be almost neurotically territorial, especially around our own parents. We were excessively sensitive to their "interference," and any suggestion from them, no matter how constructive, was regarded as a criticism.

It galled me, for instance, that my wife's parents would stuff Eric's mouth with sweets, his arms with toys, and his pockets with money. The more it galled me, of course, the more they did it. It took us years to realize that grandparents do no harm by "spoiling."

In fact, I'm now firmly convinced that it is as proper for grandparents to spoil their grandchildren as it is *improper* for parents to spoil those same children. One of the greatest pleasures of the oldest generation is making children happy, and no one has a right to interfere in that pursuit. We who are betwixt and between the innocence of childhood and the wisdom of old age, caught as we are in the complexities and grandiose seriousness of adulthood, would do well to butt out and let things be.

The rule Willie and I now apply to visits with or from grandparents is this: "When in Rome, do as the Romans do. And when the Romans come for a visit, do as the Romans do."

It makes life so much simpler.

Q: My parents live relatively close, and we see them fairly often. Spending the night with Grandma and Grandpa is a big thing for our four-year-old, who also happens to be their only grandchild. The problem is that during visits, whether we're there or not, the folks ignore our rules and let Michael do and have just about anything he wants. As a result, Michael is very hard-to-handle when we get him home, and it sometimes takes as much as several days to get things back on an even keel. How would you suggest we deal with this problem?

A: I'm going to take the grandparents' side in this one. When our children were younger, we had the same problem with Willie's parents, whom we saw fairly often. After much frustration, we finally realized that no matter what we said or did, the folks weren't going to change. We also remembered that our grandparents had treated us pretty much the same way and that we were none the worse because of it. Finally, we admitted to ourselves that when the time came, we were probably going to spoil the devil out of (or into) our grandchildren as well!

This change of attitude enabled us to realize that the control problems we were having with our children after visits with the folks weren't their fault. Blaming the children's behavior on them was buck-passing of the first magnitude. If we were willing to let the grandparents spoil the kids, then we had to take full responsibility for discipline.

Taking the bull by the horns, we sat down with the kids and told them that visits with Grandma and Grandpa were vacations from a lot of our rules, but when the visits were over, so was the vacation. Immediately after every visit, we held a transitional conversation with the kids, reminding them of our expectations. If they still had difficulty with self-control, we sent them to their rooms with instructions to remain there until they felt settled.

It wasn't long before we were truly enjoying our visits with the folks and the kids were making the transition without difficulty. Having discovered that these problems aren't the fault of grandparents, I can't wait to become one!

Q: We realize we've been much too indecisive and inconsistent with our six-year-old son. As a result, he's developed some behavior problems. How is he likely to react if we suddenly transform ourselves from parent-wimps to benevolent dictators?

A: Your child may not welcome the transformation. After all, it's going to require that he give up a significant measure of control within the family. For a time, his behavior problems are likely to escalate as he struggles to return things to the way they were. As they say, "Things get worse before they get better." If you stick to your guns, however, his behavior will improve, as will the overall relationship.

Unresolved disciplinary issues impede communication and expressions of affection between parent and child. Resolving the issues removes those impediments. It's impossible for parent and child to have truly good communication with one another until the child completely trusts and feels he can rely upon the parent's authority. As they say, the horse must always precede the cart. In this case, the horse is your authority, and the cart is an open, loving parent-child relationship.

This same is true of a teacher/student relationship. A good classroom teacher recognizes that she can teach only as effectively as she governs. So, on the first day of school, before doing anything else, she puts the horse in front of the cart by going over the rules. Realizing that some children are going to want her to prove herself, she also explains exactly what's going to happen when a child breaks a rule. When rules are broken, she follows through as promised. In so doing, she demonstrates her reliability to her students. They don't resent her for this. Quite the contrary, they trust her *because* of it.

In the long run, the happiest children are obedient children and the happiest parents are benevolent dictators. Obviously, one can't exist without the other. So, for everyone's sake, go for it!

POINT
THREE

The Roots of Responsibility

A s I travel around the country, doing talks and workshops for various parent and professional groups, I ask my audiences to participate in a small survey. I begin by asking for a show of hands to this question: "How many of you can honestly say that you *expect* your children to perform a regular routine of chores around the home for which they are not paid, with an allowance or otherwise?" In an audience of, say, five hundred, no more than fifty hands will go up.

Then: "How many of your parents would have raised their hands to the same question?" Hands go up everywhere, and people begin to laugh.

But this is really no laughing matter. It means that in the short span of one generation, we have managed to misplace a very important tenet of childrearing. Simply stated, it is that children should be *contributing* members of their families. In other words, children should have chores. There are five reasons why:

—The first is a practical one, having to do with the fact that, as I explained in Point One, the ultimate purpose of raising children is to help them out of our lives and into successful lives of their own. We have, therefore, an obligation to endow them with the skills they will need to lead successful adult lives, and domestic skills are no less important than any others that come to mind. By the age of eighteen, all children—male and female—should be familiar with and practiced at every single aspect of running a home. They should be able to wash and iron their own clothes, prepare basic meals, run a vacuum cleaner, disinfect bathrooms, replace furnace filters, mow grass, weed garden areas, and so on. They should also be responsible for earning a portion of their spending money and budgeting it sensibly. This training not only helps prepare children for adulthood, it also helps develop in them an appreciation for the effort their parents put into maintaining a household, an effort the children might otherwise take for granted.

—The second reason involves a child's sense of security. Chores *actualize* the child's participation in the family, thus strengthening feelings of acceptance and security. A child who isn't doing chores isn't participating in the family to the fullest extent possible. The child's role in the family is, therefore, a diminished one, much like that of a baseball player who, although a member of the team, rarely gets to play. Participation generates stronger feelings of membership for both the baseball player and the child.

—The third reason has to do with self-esteem. Chores enable feelings of accomplishment. Knowing that his or her contribution of time and energy to the family is regarded as important enhances a child's sense of membership in the family, enlarges upon feelings of worth, and adds immensely to self-esteem.

—The fourth reason has to do with good citizenship. In his inaugural address, President John Kennedy said, "Ask not what your country can do for you—ask what you can do for your country." In other words, a responsible citizen is one who looks more for opportunities to contribute to the system than for opportunities to take from it. No one would argue that good citizenship begins at home. Therefore, our childrearing practices should reflect this same principle. We should teach children that the reward of membership in a family comes more from what they put into the family than from what they take out of it. When this principle is turned upside-down, when children are allowed to take from the family in greater measure than their contribution justifies, their relationship to the family becomes parasitic. Inherent to this condition is a lack of motivation, perpetual self-centeredness, and the entirely false idea that something can be had for nothing.

—The fifth, and most important, reason is that chores bond a child to the values of the family. They are a child's only means of making tangible contribution to the family, and any act of contribution is, by its very nature, values-oriented. Think about it. When you make a contribution of time, money, or any other personal resource to a political, religious, educational, or charitable organization, you acknowledge two things: First, that you share values with that organization; second, that you want to do something tangible to help support and maintain those values in our society. The same applies to a child's contribution of time and energy to the family. Children who are enabled to contribute to their families on a regular basis come to a clearer understanding of their parents' values. Furthermore, they are much more likely to use those same values in their own adult lives to create success and happiness for themselves and *their* children.

The proof of what I'm saying can be found in the pudding of our country's history!

QUESTION: In what general areas or regions of this country have family values and traditions been handed down most reliably from generation to generation to generation?

ANSWER: Rural America, or more specifically, in farm country.

QUESTION: What single aspect most distinguishes the life of a child raised on a farm from that of a child raised in a city or suburban environment?

ANSWER: Chores.

That's right! As soon as they are capable, farm children are expected to perform work within their families. If they are too young to do anything but carry a milk pail, they carry a milk pail. If they are old enough to drive a tractor, they drive a tractor. And their parents don't beg, bribe, or bargain for these chores. No money changes hands (although the child may share in the profit of a certain project). There are no daily arguments over why certain work has to be done, or why a certain someone has to do it. There are no temper tantrums—no screams of "It's not fair!"—and parents don't waste time and energy on repetitious attempts at justification and explanation. These chores are simply *expected* of these children and so they get done. For a child raised on a farm, the family and its values take on importance not simply because of parental modeling and enforcement, but because the child performs a valuable function within the family. Put another way, the child is given the opportunity to *invest* in the family. When someone invests in something, that something becomes important. It becomes worthy of protecting, worthy of preserving. And so, when the farm-raised child becomes an adult, he cashes in on that investment and uses it to create success, stability, and happiness in his own life. Eventually, he passes the same lessons on to his children, realizing there is no greater gift he can possibly give them.

Willie and I didn't really begin involving Eric and Amy in housework until they were ten and seven, respectively. Until then, we had required only that they keep their rooms clean and orderly. Their growing reluctance to do anything else around the house made us finally realize the need to increase their day-to-day participation in housework.

We began by making a list of all the chores included in the housekeeping schedule, circling those we felt certain the children could handle. Lo and behold! There was, we discovered, nothing they couldn't do, and only three things—washing, ironing, and cooking—we preferred they *not* do. We listed the materials and steps involved in each chore on separate index cards and divided them into two card files, one for each child. The idea here was to leave as little as possible to the children's imaginations. Finally, we organized the schedule on two seven-day calendars which we posted on the refrigerator. The way it worked out, each child's chores took up about forty-five minutes on weekdays and two hours on Saturday.

Having put all of our "ducks in a row," we presented the plan to the children, who—believe it or not—accepted it without complaint. Well, almost. After we had explained the system, Eric looked at us and said, "What are you and Mom going to do, watch us work?" Children are so cute.

Admittedly, during the first few weeks, we had to prompt, remind, and even at times apply a little pressure. Our quality control standards were fairly strict. If one of the children failed to do a chore correctly and/or completely, he or she had to redo it. A "forgotten" chore resulted in the loss of a privilege, such as going outside to play, for a day or two. It didn't take long for the children to discover that conscientious cooperation not only took relatively little time, but also "cost" less than the alternative. Eventually, it became quite obvious they were taking considerable pride in the contribution they were making to the family. Besides all that, they learned firsthand the ins and outs of running a household, a necessary step toward helping them out of our lives. As far as Willie and I are concerned, Eric and Amy have already passed "Home Economics" with flying colors!

Any Questions So Far?

Q: At what age should parents begin assigning chores to children?

A: Three is probably the most advantageous age at which to begin assigning chores to a child. A child this age has a strong need to identify with parents and expresses that need, in part, by following them around the house, wanting to get involved in the things they're doing. If he can't get directly involved, he imitates. If Dad's repairing a leaky faucet, the child wants to help. When Mom cooks, the child gets out a few pots and pans and plays on the kitchen floor.

This interest can and should be capitalized upon by starting this-age child on a few minor chores around the home. In order to establish a routine, they should take place at the same time every day. He could, for instance, help make his bed in the morning, help set the table at dinner, and pick up his toys every evening before a bedtime story.

The feeling of accomplishment, along with the praise his parents give him for being a good helper, serves to enhance the young child's sense of belonging and thus adds significantly to his security and self-esteem.

Because threes are so eager to please, parents should have

little difficulty obtaining cooperation from them. A few chores at this age set the stage for increasing responsibilities as the child grows older. Parents are more apt to encounter resistance if they attempt to assign specific chores before age three. Likewise, a child's "chore-readiness" begins to wane if parents wait much later than four to begin acquainting him with this important facet of family life.

Q: What can parents do with children younger than three to help prepare them for a responsible role in the family?

A: Parents plant seeds of responsibility by helping younger children learn to do such things as feed themselves, dress themselves, and use the toilet. Each of these accomplishments constitutes a step toward self-sufficiency, and not only enhances the child's self-esteem but also his receptivity to additional responsibilities.

As children take these first steps toward independence, it's important that parents be more *supportive* than *directive*. In the first place, too much direction communicates the message, "You're not learning this well enough/fast enough to suit us." The child's reaction may well be to stop trying altogether. Parental overinvolvement also stifles the child's sense of accomplishment. In order for these learnings to be truly meaningful, the child must have full "ownership" of them.

When a child is ready to learn to use the toilet, for example, parents should provide a potty the child can comfortably use, training pants instead of diapers, and encouragement. Once the "props" are in place, parents should stand to the sidelines and let the process unfold, in the child's own way and at the child's own speed. The more parents hover, the more anxious they are about mistakes, the more frustrated the child will become and the longer the learning will take. This policy of supportive noninterference applies equally well to a child who's learning to feed himself, dress himself, tie his own shoes, make his bed, and even read.

Q: How much housework can parents reasonably expect of a child?

A: At the very least, a four- or five-year-old child should be responsible for keeping his room and bathroom orderly. A six-year-old can be taught to vacuum, starting with his own room. By age seven or eight, the child should be responsible for daily upkeep of his room and bathroom as well as several chores around the home. Once a week, a child this age should be required to do a major cleaning of his room and bathroom. This should include vacuuming, dusting, changing bath and bed linens, and cleaning the tub, lavatory, and commode.

A nine- to ten-year-old should contribute about forty-five minutes of "chore time" to the family on a daily basis and about two hours on Saturday. It helps to organize the daily routine into three fifteen-minute blocks. The first of these should take place first thing in the morning (straighten room and bathroom and feed the dog); the second, right after school (unload the dishwasher and put everything away); the third, after supper (clear the table, rinse dishes, scrub pots and pans, load the dishwasher, and take out the garbage).

By the way, in this scheme of things, there's no such thing as "boy-work" and "girl-work." It's all "people-work." If you are "people," then you work.

Q: Should parents pay children for chores?

A: In general, no. To begin with, payment tends to create the illusion that if the child doesn't want the money, he isn't obligated to perform the chore. Payment also dilutes the learning experience. A chore that's paid for is no longer a contribution for the sake of contribution, but a contribution for the sake of money. Paying for chores puts money in the child's pocket, but no true sense of value in the child's head. It may teach a child something about business, but nothing about the responsibility that accompanies membership in a family.

On the other hand, it's all right for parents to pay children for work above and beyond the standard routine. For instance, when Eric was in high school, I didn't pay him for mowing the lawn once a week during the summer, but I did pay him for an occasional day's work of helping me cut down trees and chop them up into fireplace logs. Even so, Eric knew that payment didn't mean the tasks were optional.

Q: Are you against giving a child an allowance?

A: Not as long as the allowance has nothing whatsoever to do with the child's chores. Chores teach responsibility, self-discipline, time-management, and a host of other essential values and skills. An allowance helps a child learn how to manage money. The two lessons should not be confused with one another. An allowance should not be used to persuade a child to carry out his chores, nor should it be suddenly withdrawn to punish him for inappropriate behavior. Parents who use money to leverage cooperation from a child are unwittingly teaching that child how to use money as a tool with which to manipulate people.

Q: When there are two children involved, wouldn't it more fair for parents to let the children alternate chores on a weekly or daily basis?

A: As fair as it may sound, an arrangement of this sort never works out. I find, in fact, that parental efforts to be fair almost always backfire.

Alternating chores inevitably results in several problems: The children end up arguing over whose turn it is to do what chores. Because none of the chores belong exclusively to either child, they take less pride in their work and do just enough to get by. When parents complain that a certain job wasn't done properly, the children point their fingers at one another. Because the chores are alternated, it takes the children longer to learn the routine. As a result, parents must constantly remind and hassle the children to get the chores done. In short, this attempt at fairness leads inevitably to frustration and conflict.

A family is an organization. As such, everyone in the family should have the equivalent of a job description. Each person's job description helps define his or her role in the family. It follows that the clearer the job description, the clearer the role. In an organization in which roles are not clear, people become frustrated and angry and the organization doesn't run smoothly. I've never heard of a business in which people exchanged jobs on a daily or weekly basis. I wouldn't recommend it for a family, either.

Responsible Behavior

Not only have today's children, by and large, not been assigned adequate responsibility within their families, they've also not been assigned adequate responsibility for their behavior—in particular, their *misbehavior*.

All too often, when a child misbehaves, parents shoulder the consequences of the problem. They take on the emotional consequences by feeling angry, frustrated, worried, embarrassed, and guilty. They take on the practical, tangible consequences by absorbing the inconveniences caused by the misbehavior. For example, they may be repeating instructions to the child more than once because the child rarely, if ever, listens the first time. They may be losing time at work because of the need to have frequent conferences with the child's teacher and/or principal. Perhaps they're repeatedly late to work because the child is never dressed and ready for school on time. They may rarely enjoy any privacy in the evening because the child fights bedtime for several hours every night.

Responsibility for a problem is measured in terms of its consequences. When parents absorb the lion's share of the emotional and tangible consequences of a child's misbehavior, they unwittingly accept responsibility for that misbehavior. In effect, the problem now belongs to them, and they will therefore try to solve it. But the harder they try, the more frustrated they will become because the *only* person who can solve it is its rightful owner, the child.

Situations of this sort call for an enactment of the "Agony Principle." It proposes: Parents should never agonize over anything a child does or fails to do if the child is perfectly capable of agonizing over it himself. In other words, when a child misbehaves, the child should be assigned both the emotional and tangible consequences of that misbehavior. Not until and unless·the "agony" of the problem rests squarely on the child's shoulders will the child be motivated to solve it.

In order to effect this transfer of responsibility from their shoulders to a child's, parents must draw upon the "Godfather Principle." First articulated by a Sicilian philosopher known as Don Corleone, the Godfather Principle simply states that in order to make a child accept responsibility for misbehavior of any sort, the child's parents must "Make him an offer he can't refuse."

A Trip to the Beach

The following true story is an illustration of the Agony and Godfather Principles at work:

In 1976, shortly after moving to Gastonia, North Carolina, the Rosemond family began taking summer vacations at Myrtle Beach, South Carolina. For the children, the trip was the event of the year, but Willie and I dreaded it. Four hours in a car with two young'uns in the throes of "We-can't wait!" might be a useful way of extracting information from P.O.W.'s, but it's no way to start a vacation.

Two minutes out of the driveway, the children would begin bickering at one another and wouldn't stop until we reached our destination. A typical exchange:

"Make Eric stop looking at me!"

"She has her feet on my side of the seat!"

"I do not! Stop pushing me! Aaaaahhhh!"

"Oh, shut up, Amy! I'm not hurting you. You're such a big baby!"

"Stop calling me names! Aaaaaahhhhh!"

And, so it went, from driveway to motel. And nothing would stop it. Not begging, not bribing, not threatening to turn around and go home. Nothing.

After suffering through several of these experiences, and while anticipating yet another, Willie and I devised a way of ending the horror forever. Our salvation came in the form of ten rectangles of colored cardboard, which we called "tickets."

When the appointed day arrived, we packed the car and then sat down with the children, "tickets" in hand.

"Kids," we said, "these are tickets. Each of you gets five of them. Hang onto them, because they're important. They have to do with the rules of riding in the car. Rule One is 'Do Not Bicker.' Rule Two is 'Do Not Make Loud Noises.' Rule Three is 'Do Not Interrupt When Mom and Dad Are Talking to Each Other.'"

"Every time you break a rule, you lose a ticket. If you bicker, you both lose a ticket, no matter who started it. Now, the first thing you want to do when you get to the beach is go in the water, right? That's where the tickets come in, because if you don't have at least one ticket left when we get to the motel, you won't be allowed in the water for two hours. During that time, you'll sit on the beach under an umbrella and watch the rest of us frolic in the surf."

We then gave out the tickets, piled in the car, and started down the road. Before we were out of the neighborhood, the kids lost their first tickets for bickering. Soon thereafter, Eric lost one for making a loud noise. Then Amy lost one for interrupting. By the time we were an hour down the road, they'd each lost four of their five tickets.

The next four hours were the quietest we'd ever spent, in or out of a car, with Eric and Amy. They said not a word to each other or to us. They clutched those last tickets to their bosoms and stared out the windows. It was the start of the best family vacation we'd ever had!

Several weeks after recounting this incident at a speaking engagement, a woman who had been in the audience called to tell me she had tried the technique, but with no success.

"The trip there was absolutely horrendous," she said, "so we decided to give your 'ticket' method a try on the way home. We gave each of the children five tickets, just like you said, and promised we would take them out for ice cream if they didn't lose all their tickets by the time we got home."

"Take them out for ice cream?" I asked.

"That's right. They're always asking us to take us out for ice cream. It's one of their favorite things. Well anyway," she continued, "they were all right for a while, then the misbe-havior started, and they proceeded to lose all their tickets in less than fifteen minutes. Then, realizing we had no control over them, they were worse than ever!"

No wonder! These parents had unwittingly violated the Godfather Principle by making their children an offer they *could* refuse! The trouble with promising a child ice cream for good behavior and then threatening to take it away for bad behavior, is that ice cream—or the lack of it—is of no real consequence. Had the children stood to lose something impor-tant, such as being able to play with their friends once they got home, the likelihood of success would have increased twenty-fold.

The Problem With Rewards

The problem with the approach these parents took is the problem with rewards in general. They rarely work. Not for long, at least.

In the first place, because they are basically "extras," re-wards are usually of minimal value to a child. Privileges such as socializing with friends or the use of a bicycle have considerable more pulling power because these are the things that define a child's *standard of living*. And just as an adult is strongly moti-vated to maintain his or her standard of living, so is a child.

In the second place, rewards are inflationary. Occasionally, a particular reward might motivate a child for a short period of time, but as soon as the child saturates on whatever reward is being used, it immediately loses its value. At this point, in order to continue motivating the child, you must increase the value of the reward.

I often tell parents that if they promise a child an ice cream cone for doing something like keeping his room clean for a week, the child will probably work to earn the reward for one or two weeks. By then, however, the novelty will have worn off and the child probably won't continue to keep his room clean for anything less than a hot fudge sundae. Within a relatively short time, hot fudge sundaes will lose their appeal, and the child's parents will again have to increase their offer. Eventually, in this family version of "Let's Make a Deal," I can envision these parents saying, "Billy, if you keep your room clean this week, we're going to send you and five of your friends to Disney World for an all-expense paid weekend, including all the ice cream you can eat!"

Absurd? Perhaps. On the other hand, I've actually heard of parents offering children things like one hundred dollars for each "A" on their report cards or two new bicycles for siblings who can manage to be "nice" to each other for a week. And sure enough, the children shape up and earn the rewards! But then, it's always back to business as usual—poor grades and constant bickering.

Rewards also prevent children from accepting responsibility for their behavior. Instead of helping a child learn that inappropriate behavior has undesirable consequences, rewards can result in the child developing a manipulative, "What's in it for me?" attitude toward appropriate behavior. In other words, instead of learning that good behavior is rewarding in and of itself, the child learns to use the promise of good behavior as a bargaining tool to get new toys, privileges, and other "goodies."

Not long ago, I explained the risks of using rewards to a gathering of parents in Miami. Afterwards, a mother approached me and thanked me for my remarks. She said, "I've used rewards a lot because I was under the impression that they helped promote good self-esteem. Now I understand why every time I take my child anywhere, he asks, 'If I'm good, will you buy me a new toy?'"

An occasional spontaneous reward, used as an acknowledgment of achievement or progress in a certain area, is fine. Rewards that haven't been contracted for are more sincere and, therefore, more effective at promoting both good behavior and good self-esteem. Children should, of course, be praised for their accomplishments, but even praise is most effective when it's low-key and occasional.

In the Question-and-Answer portion of this chapter, we'll look at several other specific examples of how the "Agony" and "Godfather" Principles can be used to assign responsibility for a problem to a child.

Running After the Bus

Several years ago, while I was in Kansas City speaking at a convention of city managers, I found myself on the same bill with Tom Peters and Robert Waterman, the authors of *In Search of Excellence*, the best-selling book about corporate management. Because they were scheduled immediately before me, I had the pleasure of hearing most of their presentation.

At one point during their talk, they flashed the letters MBWA on the screen behind them and explained that this was not a new graduate degree they'd invented, but stood for a concept they called "Management by Wandering Around." That set off peals of laughter. Peters and Waterman then surprised the audience by announcing that MBWA was perhaps the most efficient and motivating of all management styles.

They said that managers who practice MBWA are skilled at delegating responsibility, and equally skilled at staying out of the way of the people to whom they delegate. They are authority figures who make their knowledge and expertise available to the people they supervise, but they do not hover over the people who work for them, watching their every move.

They trust that their staff can and will do their jobs properly and communicate that trust by not becoming overly involved in their work. They motivate people by giving them responsibility, along with the opportunity to discover the intrinsic rewards of independent achievement. By wandering instead of bustling anxiously around, they create a relaxed work environment, one in which people are free to be as creative and productive as they are capable. In effect, instead of being "bosses" in the traditional sense of the term, managers who wander around are *consultants* to the people they supervise. Their general policy is one of noninterference, and they break with this rule only if absolutely necessary. They are role models, teachers, guidance counselors, gurus.

Listening to and absorbing what Peters and Waterman were saying about the "new manager," it occurred to me that MBWA applied to raising children as well as to managing adults. The most effective parents, I realized, are those who are not constantly busy in their children's lives, but are relaxed and therefore create a relaxed environment in which their children can discover their potential. Instead of hovering anxiously over their children, they act as consultants to their growth and development.

Parents of this sort are authority figures, but they guide and model more than they order. Their goal is not to make their children subservient or dependent, but to make them independent and responsible. Toward this end, they provide a variety of opportunities for growth, but allow their children a great deal of freedom when it comes to choosing or rejecting those opportunities.

Instead of taking credit when their children behave well, and feeling guilty when their children behave poorly, they assign to their children responsibility, both positive and negative, for their own behavior. Above all else, they let their children make mistakes, realizing that some of the most valuable lessons in life can only be learned through trial-and-error. In all these ways, they send messages of trust and personal worth to their children, who are free to discover their capacities for love and creativity. In effect, these rare but wonderful parents practice the all-but-lost art of "Parenting by Wandering Around."

It is unfortunate that there are not more parents who wander around. I am thinking in particular of well-intentioned parents who insist upon becoming too involved in their children's lives. Because they live through their children, they take their children's successes and failures very seriously and very personally. They *over*-direct, *over*-structure, *over*-protect, and *over*-indulge. They take on responsibility that rightfully belongs to their children, thus robbing them of opportunities for growth.

Several years ago, I came across an article in the *Hartford Courant* written by Nancy Davis, a teacher of journalism at Miss Porter's School in Farmington, Connecticut. She wrote, ". . . the advice that children need to try and fail, with supportive parents behind them, is hard for parents to take. We want to spare them the failures, big and small, which we experienced or which we see looming on their horizons. We've been told a hundred times that people learn from their mistakes, but we want our children to never make mistakes because they may be hurt in the process."

Davis's advice to parents was simply, "Don't run after the bus." Those five words capture the essence of good parenting better than any five I've heard in a long time. Thank you, Tom Peters and Robert Waterman, and thank you, Nancy Davis.

The Sound of Face Striking Pavement

A mother recently asked what she could do to get her six-year-old son to keep his shoes tied.

"I know this must sound silly," she said, "but every time I look at him, his shoelaces are flopping all over the place. It's driving me nuts!"

"Why do you want him to keep his shoelaces tied?" I asked.

"Well," she answered, "besides looking bad, he's going to trip over them someday."

"And what's the worst thing that could happen if he tripped?"

She thought for a moment. "He might fall and hurt himself."

"Badly?" I asked.

"Probably not," she answered.

"But perhaps badly enough to think twice the next time he leaves his shoelaces untied?" I offered.

After a thoughtful pause, she answered, "Maybe."

"Then I suggest you do nothing at all. Let his shoelaces flop. Let him learn the hard way."

The hard way—my dad used that phrase a lot. "There are certain things I can't teach you," he would say. "You're going to have to learn them the way everyone else does—the hard way."

In retrospect, I realize Dad was, once again, right on the mark. Some of the most valuable lessons in my life have been learned courtesy of falling flat on my face.

By and large, today's parent seems to think that letting a child fall flat on his face when the fall could have been intercepted, or even prevented altogether, is not only irresponsible, but downright cruel. The prevailing attitude has it that if you, the parent, see the fall coming and do nothing to prevent it, then *you* are responsible for the results, not the child.

Cedric won't do his homework, so every evening his parents sit down with him and see that it gets done. Whenever Angel has a conflict with another child in the neighborhood, her mother runs interference, calling the other child's parents, making sure things are set right for Angel. To prevent him from falling in with the "wrong crowd," Rodney's parents censor his choice of friends. Englebert's parents take him to a different after-school activity every day of the week and Saturday morning to make sure he stays "active."

I call this sort of obsessive hovering "Parenting by Helicopter," the upshot of which is that many of today's children never learn to accept responsibility for their behavior because their parents are doing a fine job of accepting that responsibility for them. But responsibility isn't the only thing at stake.

Almost all learning is accomplished through trial-and-error. Therefore, if you prevent the error, you prevent the learning. By making mistakes, one learns what works and what doesn't. Eventually, after a period of failure, the person fine-tunes his or her skills and masters the task at hand.

Standing back and letting that failure occur, in a supportive but noninterfering way, gives a child room to develop initiative, resourcefulness, and numerous problem-solving skills. It also lets the child come to grips with the frustration inherent to the learning of any skill—social, academic, emotional, and so on. That's how children learn to persevere, and perseverance—as we all know from experience—is the main ingredient in *every* success story.

It all boils down to this: If we want our children to stand on their own two feet, we must also be willing to let them fall. So let's stop tying their shoelaces.

Making Amends

Having to accept responsibility for one's own behavior develops self-control. Since the purpose of discipline is to teach self-control, then any method of discipline, if it is to be effective, must assign responsibility for the child's behavior to the child. Simply put, when a child does something bad, he should feel bad about it, and be required to take whatever steps are necessary to correct it. This is how conscience develops.

Unfortunately, many of today's children don't enjoy the advantages of this process. All too often, when a child does something wrong, his parents wind up feeling bad about it and making the compensation. Thus protected from the consequences of his behavior, the child grows not in responsibility and self-control, but in irresponsibility and self-centeredness.

There is a general tendency among adults to feel that when a child misbehaves, the child should be punished. That's sometimes true, but equally true is the fact that punishment sometimes misses the point. When a child's misbehavior is hurtful to someone else, for example, it's more important that the child make amends than that the child be punished.

A number of years ago, an upset neighbor called to tell us that Amy, then eight, had been disrespectful toward her. The implication in her outrage was that we must be bad parents for having such a bad child.

When she'd finished venting her anger, I said, "Let me assure you of several things. First, I believe what you're telling me. Second, I agree that what Amy did was completely inappropriate and that there is no excuse for it. Third, I'm grateful to you for letting me know and for being so honest about your feelings. Fourth, Amy will correct the problem she's created. Last, but not least, I want you to feel free to call any time you see one of our children doing something wrong."

There was a long period of silence on the other end of the line. Finally, in an almost apologetic tone, the neighbor said, "Well, now you know, Amy is usually a very good little girl. This is the only time she's ever given me trouble."

"I'm glad to hear that," I said, "but that doesn't excuse or erase what she's done."

When the conversation ended, I found Amy and confronted her with the neighbor's report. "I'm very unhappy about this, Amy," I said. "You do not have permission to be disrespectful to *any* adult, under *any* circumstances."

She started to cry. A good sign, I thought to myself. But just feeling bad about what she'd done wasn't going to correct the mistake.

"I've decided that you're going to apologize to Mrs. So-and-So for your disrespect."

Amy immediately became very agitated. "Oh, please, Daddy. Don't make me do that. Make me stay inside and don't let me play with my friends, or take my toys away, but don't make me go over there and apologize, please, Daddy, please!"

"Sorry, kid, but this isn't open for discussion."

"Can I call her on the phone?"

"No, you'll do it face-to-face."

"Will you go with me?"

"No, Amy, I won't. I didn't help you create the problem, and I won't help you solve it. And that, little girl, is my final word on the subject."

When she realized I wasn't going to budge, she composed herself, walked across the street, rang the doorbell, and apologized. As I watched from the living room window, I saw the neighbor smile, take Amy's hand in hers, and nod as if to say that everything was all right.

Amy came back across the street with tears streaming down her face. There were no more punishments, no more lectures. In fact, we never again made mention of the situation.

Sometimes, when I tell this story or another like it, a listener will remark that it sounds as if I'm in favor of "laying guilt trips" on children. To a certain extent, I am.

When a child does something wrong, she should feel the wrong of what she's done. The only way to communicate that feeling is through the child's emotional system. In other words, just telling a child she did wrong isn't usually enough. The words you use must come across with enough impact to make the child feel guilty or embarrassed or sorry, or all those things.

The phrase, "guilt trip," carries lots of negative connotations, and guilt can certainly be used in sadistic, hostile ways. At its extremes, guilt is maladaptive. People who are incapable of feeling guilt are called "sociopaths." They do what they please without regard for anyone else, or remorse for whatever hurt they might cause. On the other hand, people who carry around excessive feelings of guilt are "neurotic." They are constantly haunted by the idea that they're doing something wrong. But guilt can also be a very adaptive emotion. Without it, civilization as we know it wouldn't exist. People won't accept responsibility for their own bad behavior unless they feel bad about it. Guilt is a message from inside that says we misbehaved and shouldn't behave that way again. The idea that guilt, all guilt, is bad, came out of the "Do Your Own Thing" philosophy of the sixties and seventies. Well, it's high time we got our heads out of the clouds and planted our parenting attitudes in the soil of common sense.

Our job as parents is to socialize our children. You can't teach a child how to act without also teaching her how to think and how to feel. Children won't know to feel guilty unless we first teach them that guilt is appropriate to certain situations. That's how a child's conscience develops. Once you've taught a child the basics, you can then trust her to come to feelings of guilt on her own, when those feelings are appropriate. Even so, there may be times, such as was the case with Amy and the neighbor, when parents will need to drive the point home.

Empathy vs. Sympathy

I frequently encourage parents to stop sympathizing with their children's problems and begin empathizing with them instead. They often tell me they didn't know there was a difference.

But there is, and it's a big one. Empathy involves understanding, and sends the message, "What are you going to do about it?" Sympathy, on the other hand, involves pampering, and sends the message, "Oh, you poor thing! You haven't done anything to deserve this!" Sympathy is like custard. The longer you stir it, the thicker and stickier it gets. Eventually, it does more to hinder change than help it.

When a child is having personal problems, a little sympathy can sometimes help open lines of communication. But, sympathy has a quickly reached point of diminishing returns. Stir too much into a situation, and you're likely to create more problems than you solve.

Why? Because, like morphine, sympathy in small amounts eases pain, but in large amounts, it's addictive. And once addicted, the child stops trying to solve problems and starts trying to get more and more sympathy. Since a problem has to exist in order for the child to get sympathy, problems begin to accumulate as the child settles ever more passively and comfortably into the role of "victim."

When Eric entered junior high, he began having problems getting along with peers. At first, he complained of being picked on, then that other kids were trying to get him in trouble, then that he had no friends. Initially, we regarded his complaints with a grain of salt, thinking they were nothing more than temporary problems of adjustment. As time went on, however, things went from bad to worse. We noticed that he rarely received phone calls, that he spent weekend nights at home, and that he was looking and acting increasingly depressed. On occasion, we'd hear him crying in his room. Alarmed, we started asking questions. Out came the most horrendous tale of woe we'd ever heard.

There was a group of kids at school, he said, who were not only making fun of him, but also spreading rumors that he was, well, let's just say "different." He was being ostracized by the other boys and ignored by the girls. One particular group of boys had even written an obscene note to a girl and signed Eric's name. For that, he was grilled by the principal, who ended up satisfied that Eric had nothing to do with the note. Nonetheless, the incident left its mark on the little guy's self-confidence.

We knew junior-high kids were capable of sadistic cruelty, but this seemed beyond belief. So, we sympathized. We talked, we counseled, we comforted, we even cried with him. We tried building him up by telling him what a really wonderful person he was and that his tormentors wouldn't turn out half as well. We did everything we could think of to let him know how unfair we thought the whole mess was. But things just kept getting worse. He moped constantly, he never went out, and the tales of woe became more and more woeful. Finally, we realized that Eric was suffering as much from an overdose of sympathy as he was from anything else. Our good intentions had whipped a relatively small flame into a forest fire.

Finally, we sat down with him and said, "Look, kid, we feel for you and all, but we've noticed of late that you aren't doing anything to solve these problems. It's almost like you're beginning to enjoy this little soap opera. So, we've decided there are going to be no more conversations about your social problems. We've said all there is to say about them. Now, it's time for you to get yourself in gear and do something about them. We're giving you three weeks in which to find a friend and start doing things with him. If you haven't done anything by then, we'll take matters in hand and begin calling some parents ourselves to see if we can arrange some activities. In other words, either you do it, or we will."

The threat of embarrassment was a gentle, but adequate, boot in the rear. In two weeks, he had a friend. Within a year, he had more friends than he could keep up with.

That's the difference.

It's Never Too Late

· In order for children to become successful at the three Rs of reading, 'riting, and 'rithmetic, their parents must first teach them the three Rs of respect, responsibility, and resourcefulness.

After explaining this concept to a group of professional educators in Phoenix, a teacher approached me to ask, "Can something still be done for a fourteen-year-old whose parents, until now, have failed to teach your three Rs?"

"I'm convinced it's never too late," I replied, "but in order to reverse a situation with that much history and momentum behind it, the youngster's parents are going to have to do the very thing they've been afraid to do for fourteen years."

"Which is?" she asked.

"Make him unhappy," I said.

It's never too late. The personality of a child is not, contrary to myth, carved in stone by age six, or sixteen for that matter. In fact, it remains flexible, and therefore malleable, well through adolescence.

Even as adults, significant events and relationships continue to mold the personality for as long as the individual is receptive to change. In the final analysis, the ability to change is a matter of choice, not chronology. The problem is that a teenager in need of "attitude adjustment" isn't likely to recognize the need. Since he isn't going to make the decision, someone needs to make it for him.

Once the decision has been made, the first step is that of getting the teenager's attention. The only way to do this is to confront the teen with full responsibility for his/her behavior. Since responsibility is measured in terms of consequences, this means the parents must stop whatever they're doing to protect the youngster from consequences.

I'm talking about a crash course in reality. This kind of emergency action demands commitment, consistency, and a complete lack of sympathy for the child's sudden plight. In addition, the parents need to let go of guilt—whether real or imagined—for past mistakes. Actually, sympathy and guilt go hand in hand. Guilt—the idea that "if I'd been a better parent, he'd be a better person"—drives sympathetic responses, which, in turn, generate compensatory behavior.

For the confrontation to succeed, parents must stop blaming themselves (dwelling in the past) and charge strategically ahead toward their objectives (focus on the future). Now, it stands to reason that, when you confront the irresponsible youth with reality, unhappiness will be the inevitable result.

The problem is that most parents don't like to make their children unhappy. They seem to think that the evidence of good parenting is a happy child. It follows, therefore, that if the child is unhappy, the parents must be doing something wrong.

Absurd? You bet! But powerful, nonetheless.

For example, the parents of an unmotivated tenth grader might insist that, every Friday, he must bring home a progress report signed (in ink) by every one of his teachers. To have freedom, all of the teachers must indicate better-than-passing work. If not, or if the report is incomplete or doesn't find its way home, then the youngster has no freedom until the following Friday, when another chance to "pass inspection" is granted.

The heretofore irresponsible teen will greet these requirements with (a) rage, (b) refusal, (c) plea bargaining, (d) all of the above. In other words, unhappiness.

The story is likely to last, with brief periods of deceptive calm, for three months or more. But if the parents will batten down the hatches and hang dispassionately in there, it will eventually subside and a new day of understanding will dawn in that child's life.

You see, sometimes unhappiness is not only the best form of therapy, but also the only form possible.

Questions?

Q: Every morning, our seven-year-old drags his feet about getting out of bed and getting dressed. Both my husband and I work, and this requires that Billy leaves the house no later than 7:45 A.M. We wake him up at 6:30, which gives him more than enough time to get ready for school. Every morning, it's the same story. We have to call him five or six times to get him up and moving, then we have to stay behind him until he's out the door. Help!

A: First, the only person who can solve this problem is Billy. Second, he's not going to solve it until you make him responsible for it. Third, he has no reason to accept responsibility for the problem as long as you are willing to continue accepting it for him. Billy will solve the problem when, and only when, his failure to get up and get moving in the morning upsets and inconveniences *him* more than it upsets and inconveniences you.

The actual mechanics of the solution are as easy as A-B-C:

A: Plan your strategy. In Chapter 2, I called this "Striking While the Iron Is Cold." Make a detailed list of the things you want Billy to do in the morning.

B: Communicate the plan to Billy. Say, "Billy, we've decided we're no longer going to yell and scream and get red in the face in the mornings. From now on, after waking you up at 6:30, we're going down to the kitchen and set the stove timer for 7:15. That gives you forty-five minutes to do the things you see on this list, which we're going to post on the back of your bedroom door. When the timer rings, we're going to hold inspection. If everything on the list has been done, and done properly, you may do whatever you like until it's time to leave the house. If, on the other hand, you either fail to beat the bell or haven't properly done one or more things on the list, you won't be allowed to go outside after school that day. In addition, your bedtime that night will be one hour earlier than usual. Any questions?"

C: Enforce the plan. When Billy dawdles, as he will, say and do nothing. Between 6:30 and 7:15 every morning, your job is to tend to your business and ignore whether or not Billy is attending to his. I guarantee he will fail to beat the bell at least two or three mornings the first week. He may even still be in bed when the bell rings. If that happens, get him ready without fuss or frenzy (thus the thirty-minute "cushion" built into the plan). That afternoon, if he starts outside, gently remind him of his self-imposed restriction and express your regrets. When he pleads for "One more chance!" say, "Sorry Billy, but you knew the rule." When Billy realizes that the problem is his to do with as he pleases, he will solve it. He may be stubborn, but he's not stupid.

Q: I have a problem that is slowly driving me crazy. My two boys, ages ten and eight, bicker at one another constantly. To make matters worse, after nearly every fracas, it's a game of who can get to Mom first with the most dramatic rendition of "Poor, poor, pitiful me!" I know I shouldn't referee, but if I ignore them, the fighting only gets louder. If you don't have any good ideas, then at least do me the favor of referring me to a contractor who specializes in custom-designed rubber rooms. I'm soon going to need one.

A: Actually, you're not refereeing as much as you are emceeing a game of "Victim, Victim, Who's the Victim?" Unfortunately, even though your intentions are good, and your motives certainly understandable, by making the distinction between "villain" and "victim," you seal the inevitability of further conflict. You see, the children aren't coming to you because they fight. They fight because you let them come to you.

When you get involved in their squabbles, you assign to one

child the role of victim, and to the other the role of villain. In this upside-down set of circumstances, the victim "wins" because Mom is on his side. So, the children begin competing to be the victim. In effect, by getting involved in their bickering, you are teaching them that there is something desirable about being downtrodden. If one of the children wins by losing often enough, perhaps he will earn the coveted "Victim for Life" award. A dubious distinction, indeed! To get them to stop playing this dangerous game, you must transfer responsibility for the problem from your shoulders to theirs.

You can use the "Countdown to Confinement" method. Call a conference with the children and say something along these lines: "Guess what, kids? Mom's figured out a way for the two of you to fight all you want without driving me crazy! I call it "Problem, Problem, Now You Have the Problem!" From now on, every time you guys bicker, fight, tattle, or are rude to one another, I'm going to confine you to your respective rooms for thirty minutes. It won't matter who started the problem, who was being unfair, or whatever. Regardless of who supposedly started it, you will both spend thirty minutes in your room. I'm no longer going to play "Who Done It?" with the two of you. Now listen carefully, because the third time I have to send you to your rooms on any given day it won't be for thirty minutes. It will be for the rest of the day. You will be allowed out only to use the bathroom and to eat meals with the family.

"Oh, yes, there's one more thing. You're used to hearing me threaten, but you're not used to having me follow through on a threat. This time, I'm not threatening. I'm promising. But you'll have to find that out for yourselves."

Now, instead of fighting with one another for the purpose of getting you involved, the children must learn how to cooperate in order to keep you from getting involved. Aren't you clever?

Q: I'm having a problem getting my four-year-old to go to bed and stay there. I put her to bed, she gets up a few minutes later to ask for a glass of water. I give her a glass of water and put her back to bed, she gets up three minutes later to ask me something like, "When's Christmas?" I answer her question and put her back to bed, and she gets up a few minutes later and wants to know what I'm doing. This sometimes goes on for an hour or more. Eventually, I blow my top, then she starts to cry, and I feel bad. At that point, the game starts all over again. What can I do?

A: First, make a "doorknob thing" out of cardboard. You know, one of those "Do Not Disturb" signs that hangs on hotel room doorknobs. On one side, draw a circle and color it green. Draw another circle on the other side and color it red.

Put your daughter to bed at the same time every night. As you leave her room, hang the doorknob thing on her doorknob with the "green light" showing. The green light means that she can get out of bed one time. When she does, answer her question or whatever and put her back in bed. This time, as you leave her room, turn the doorknob thing over so that the "red light" is now showing.

Say, "A red light means 'STOP!' This red light means you may not come out of your room again this evening. If you do, you'll stay inside tomorrow and go to bed one hour early."

When she "runs the red light," take her immediately back to her room and put her back in bed. Don't answer any questions and don't respond to any further requests. She will undoubtedly continue to get out of bed. Just continue putting her back in. Remember that it takes a child time to develop a habit, and likewise, time to catch the cure. The next day, as promised, keep her inside and put her to bed an hour early and go through the same procedure.

She'll probably run the red light several nights in a row. Then, she'll catch on and you'll have a couple of successful bedtimes. Remember, if she obeys the red light, she gets to go outside the next day and her usual bedtime is restored. Over the next few weeks, expect to go two steps forward and then a step back. She should start cooperating consistently with bedtime within two to four weeks. Regardless, keep using the doorknob-thing procedure every night for at least three months. It will take at least that much time for the new habit to fully develop.

Q: Our fourteen-year-old daughter's room is an absolute disaster! The floor is littered with record albums, clothes, magazines, and other personal belongings. Her bed is never made (unless I make it) and all of her drawers are usually open. She maintains that because it's her room, she should be allowed to keep it any way she likes. She's also started closing herself up in there for hours at a time to talk to friends on her phone. If we ask her to spend time with the family, she looks at us as if we're crazy and asks, "Why?" To tell you the truth, we haven't come up with a good answer. What should we do?

A: If your daughter is anything like our daughter Amy was at that age, you won't be able to get her out of her room with a crowbar. Today's kids go into their rooms when they hit thirteen and stay there until they get drivers' licenses. I'm convinced it's a preparatory ritual of some sort. In any case, believe me, it's best. If they grace the family with more than five minutes of their presence, you want them back in their rooms anyhow.

The room itself is another matter. This stuff about "It's my room and I should be able to keep it any way I like," is hogwash. Her room is in *your* house, and the standard of cleanliness you set should be the standard she follows. She won't appreciate the value of an orderly, clean environment until you've "convinced" her to live in one for a while. Talking to her about this will only make you blue in the face.

Make a rule: Every morning, before she leaves for school, she must make her bed, straighten her room, and close her drawers. After she's gone, you inspect. If her room's neat and relatively clean, she gets to keep her phone. If it's not, you impound it, in which case the phone stays with you until room check the next morning.

Saturday becomes major room-cleaning day, which means she must vacuum, dust, and change her sheets in addition to putting everything in its place and straightening her drawers. Put her weekend life on "hold"—no phone, no social life—until this has been done, and done properly. When she says she's finished, check her work. If you open a drawer, and it's crammed with junk, just say, "You have some more work to do," and walk out. Slowly but surely, she'll learn to appreciate having a clean room.

Just another example of the Godfather Principle in action. Thank you, Don Corleone!

Q: Our twelve-year-old son has always been well-behaved, responsible, and honest. This year, he started junior high school and began hanging around with several kids who are troublemakers. As soon as we found out, we forbade the association. He says we're trying to choose his friends and seems determined to disobey. It's the first really major conflict we've ever had, and quite frankly, it's a bit scary. What should we do?

A: Nothing. This is actually a great opportunity for both you and your son to learn some very important lessons. You can learn to let go, to stop being so protective. In turn, he can learn to be more responsible for the choices he makes. None of you are going to learn anything, however, unless you allow him the freedom to make certain mistakes.

Learning generally takes place by trial-and-error. This means that many attempts and many mistakes must be made before a particular skill is truly mastered. If the learner is prevented from making mistakes, the learning won't ever take place. This applies to learning to hit a baseball or drive a car as well as to making good decisions.

We can all recall making a decision that brought us face-to-face with the pavement. Instead of wallowing in self-pity, we picked ourselves up, dusted ourselves off, and carried on, slightly scarred perhaps, but a whole lot wiser. Looking back, we realize that even if someone had warned us we were headed for a fall, we'd probably have fallen anyway. These painfully learned lessons are necessary to growing up and learning to accept the consequences—good or bad—of the choices we make.

You should not only let your son associate with these boys, you should actually hope and pray he *does* get into trouble with them. Let's face it, the worst that could happen at this age isn't likely to ruin his, or anyone else's, life. Let your son make his mistakes with these boys and, as a result, learn to pick his friends more carefully.

Tell him this: "You were right. We *have* been trying to choose your friends. We'd really rather you didn't hang around with those boys, but we're no longer going to try to prevent it.

"Whether you influence them in right directions or they influence you in wrong directions is up to you. But, hear this! If you get into any trouble with them, not only will you never again be allowed to associate with them, but there will also be a significant period of time in your life when you won't be allowed to associate with anyone. You have the freedom you want, but you'd better take care of it, because along with that freedom comes a lot of responsibility."

Make it clear that if he should happen to get into trouble, you're going to hold him completely responsible for his own behavior. You will not give *any* consideration to such excuses as "It wasn't my idea," or "I didn't do anything but stand and watch," or "They told me if I didn't help, they'd beat me up."

If he wants to bring these boys home with him, welcome them into your home. Who knows? Maybe your example will open their eyes to a better set of values.

Q: Our son started sixth grade this year. He's always had a problem taking responsibility for his homework. As a result, his father and I have had to make sure he kept up with his assignments. When I went to talk with his teacher about the problem, she politely told me to stay out of it. She would take care of it, she said. With more than a little trepidation, I agreed. Unfortunately, Andrew is abusing his freedom. Most of the work I've seen has been hurriedly done. When I pointed this out to the teacher, she calmly told me she and Andrew were "working things out" and for me not to worry. Hah! I'm not supposed to worry while I see my son's grades go down the tube?

A: You've discovered the truth in the adage, "Things get worse before they get better." In fact, I'm convinced that not only *do* things get worse, they virtually *must*.

When parents assume responsibility for a problem that rightfully belongs to a child, they end up compensating for the problem without truly correcting it. These compensations have the unintended effect of allowing the child to stay irresponsible. In your case, you've taken it upon yourselves to do for Andrew what he should have been doing for himself. You've made sure he brought his books home; you've stood over him, figuratively or otherwise, while he did his homework; you've checked to make sure the work was up to par.

You've been doing what many golfers do when they develop

a slice. Instead of correcting the defect in their swing that causes the ball to curve maddeningly to the right, they compensate by aiming to the left of their target. In so doing, the problem doesn't get solved, but the consequences of it become less noticeable. In fact, the compensation makes the problem *worse* because it gives the slice time to become habit. The longer the golfer compensates for it, the harder it is to solve.

Like the golfer, you've been "aiming further left." As a result, Andrew has learned to rely on you to take up the slack in his academic life. And, like our golfer friend, your compensations have succeeded in making Andrew's problem less noticeable. He's still irresponsible, but his grades don't show it.

If the golfer stops aiming left, his next ten shots will go in the woods. In other words, as soon as he stops compensating for it, the problem will seem to get worse. But, by making the problem more noticeable, it finally becomes possible to correct it.

Likewise, Andrew's teacher realizes that in order for him to begin taking responsibility for himself, you're going to have to stop taking responsibility for him. Having done what she told you to do, you're in a panic because the problem is now more noticeable and all your past accomplishments seem to be going down the tubes. But that's just the point. The accomplishments were *yours*, not his. It's time Andrew learned to walk on his own two feet. As he does, he's bound to stumble and perhaps even fall flat on his face. That's all right. He seems blessed with a teacher who sees the problem and knows how to solve it. Trust her. She sounds like the answer to a prayer.

POINT
FOUR

The Fruits of Frustration

*F*rustration, said nearly an entire generation of childrearing experts (circa 1950 to the present), is bad for children. It causes stress, insecurity, and poor self-esteem, they said, not to mention warts on the vocal chords from too much screaming. Believing in this fairy tale, parents worked hard to protect their children from this supposedly terrible scourge. In the process, they gave their children too much, too soon, and generally required too little, too late. As a result, children became increasingly spoiled, demanding, and ungrateful, while parents became increasingly frustrated. Just goes to show, what goes around comes around.

I have good news! Those childrearing experts were wrong! Frustration isn't necessarily bad for children. In fact, a certain amount is absolutely *essential* to healthy character formation and emotional growth.

You want proof? Here 'tis:

—As pointed out in Point One, the purpose of raising children is to help them out of our lives and into successful lives of their own. Parents are therefore obligated to raise children in a manner consistent with the reality they will eventually face as adults. Are you with me so far?

—As we all know, adult reality involves significant amounts of frustration. We experience frustration in response to not only our own limitations, but also the limitations other people and circumstances impose upon us.

—Through experience with frustration we eventually develop a tolerance for it. We accept its inevitability and determine not to let it get us down. This tolerance enables the growth of resourcefulness and other creative coping mechanisms. People who learn to tolerate frustration are able to turn adversity into challenge and persevere in the face of it.

—Perseverance, that all-important, "if at first you don't succeed, try and try again" attitude toward life, is the primary quality in *every* success story. Whether the field of endeavor be occupational, recreational, social, personal, marital, or parental, the person who perseveres is the person most likely to succeed.

—All of the aforementioned growth takes place *because of*— not in spite of—that supposedly dreadful f-word, "frustration."

Conclusion: If you want your children to become successful adults—successful in their work, their play, their interpersonal relationships, and their feelings toward themselves—you are obligated to frustrate them.

If you aren't doing so already, you can begin tending to this obligation by giving your children regular, daily doses of Vitamin N. This vital nutrient consists simply of the most character-building two-letter word in the English language. Vitamin N is as important to a child's healthy growth and development as Vitamins A, B, and C. Unfortunately, many, if not most, of today's children suffer from Vitamin N deficiency. They've been overindulged by well-meaning parents who've given them far too much of what they want and far too little of what they truly need.

A Self-Test

Have you given your children enough Vitamin N? Let's find out. List on a sheet of paper everything you've ever dreamed of having. Let your imagination and your greed run unabashedly wild! Don't concern yourself with whether these things are practical or presently affordable, whether your spouse shares your dreams, or whether your minister would approve of them. If you've ever coveted a particular something, write it down! What about that German sports car you've always wanted? And how about a new house? Don't hold back! You want new furniture? Write it down! A new wardrobe? A boat? Jewelry? A trip to Europe? A membership at the country club? A hot tub? Write 'em down!

When your fantasy-frenzy is over, let reality intrude. Go back over your wish-list and circle the things you feel reasonably certain you'll actually be able to acquire within the next five years. When I put a workshop audience through the same exercise, the answers generally fall between 10 and 20 percent. If you circle more than 25 percent of the items on your list, you're either incredibly wealthy or you don't want much. In other words, most of us must learn to contend with the fact that from 10 to 20 percent of what we want today is about as much as we can hope to acquire within five years. Remember, too, that we get what we want by putting forth sustained effort, by making sacrifices, by doing our best. And through it all, we endure all manner of . . . what? That's right! Frustration! Now you're catching on!

Now, on a second sheet of paper, list everything your children are going to ask for over the next twelve months. Not things they truly need, mind you, but things they simply want—the extras. Depending on their ages, they're going to want toys of every description, various items of electronic equipment, various means of fancy transportation, the latest in a never-ending cycle of clothing fads, and the cost of admission to movies, sports events, amusement parks, and rock 'n roll concerts.

When you're through, go back over that second list, circling the things your children are probably or definitely going to get within the next twelve months. Don't forget to circle things that are probably forthcoming from grandparents, other well-meaning relatives, and friends of the family. Eye-opening, isn't it? If you're a typical American parent, you circled 75 percent or more of the items on your children's wish-list.

What this means is that most of us accustom our children to a material standard that is completely out of kilter with what they can ever hope to achieve as adults. Consider also that many, if not most of them, attain this level of affluence not by working, sacrificing, or doing their best, but by whining, demanding, and manipulating. So, in the process of over-inflating their materialistic expectations, we also teach our children that something can be had for next to nothing. Not only is that a falsehood, it's one of the most dangerous, destructive attitudes a person can ever acquire.

Children who grow up believing in the something-for-nothing fairy tale may never realize that the really important things in life come from within, rather than without. As adults, they are likely to be emotionally stunted, immature people, fixated at a grasping, self-centered stage of development. At the very least, they will tend to confuse the giving and getting of *things* with a deeper and more meaningful level of sharing and trust in relationships. When they themselves become parents, they're likely to confuse their children's value systems in a like manner, by overdosing them with things. In this sense, materialism is an inherited disease, an addiction passed from one generation to the next. But materialism is not so much an addiction to *things* as it is an addiction to *acquiring* things. This explains why a materialist is never content. No sooner than he's acquired one thing, he wants another. This also explains why children who get too much of what they want rarely take care of anything they have. Why should they? After all, history tells them that more is on the way.

Our children deserve better than this. They deserve, first, to have us attend conscientiously to their needs for protection, affection, and direction. Beyond that, they deserve to hear us say "no" far more often than "yes" when it comes to their whimsical yearnings. They deserve to learn that getting requires giving in at least equal measure. They need to learn not just the words, but the deeper meaning behind the words, "It is better to give than to receive." They deserve to learn the value of constructive, creative effort, as opposed to the value of effort expended whining, lying on the floor kicking and screaming, or playing one parent against the other. They deserve to learn that work is the *only* truly fulfilling way of getting anything in life.

In effect, in the process of trying to protect our children from frustration, we've turned reality upside-down and inside-out. The problem is that a child raised in this topsy-turvy manner may not, when the time comes, have the skills needed to stand on his or her own two feet.

In Pursuit of Happiness

Four years after graduating from high school, 42 percent of the class of 1980 were still "nesting" under their parents' roofs, compared with just 25 percent of the class of 1972. A 68 percent increase in eight years!

You'd think one reason all these young people stay unmarried and continue to live at home is so they can accumulate a nest egg, but that's not the case. The same study found that they save less and spend more than any previous generation. The fact is, most of these young people were raised by parents who gave them lots of material things but required little in return. Having grown up in a blissful state of premature affluence, these kids can't handle the relative hardship of being out on their own. So they stay at home, which frees up lots of income for discretionary things like new cars, expensive stereo equipment, and ski trips. In other words, their childhood experience of how the world works has failed to prepare them for self-sufficiency. They aren't willing to start small, to struggle, to sacrifice, to hang in there.

By and large, today's children have not only been overdosed materially, but emotionally as well. They've been given too much attention, too much praise, and too many rewards. In short, we've made their lives too easy, and in so doing, we've created a fantasy of how the world works. I recently spoke with another family therapist who summed up the situation quite well. He said, "This generation of parents has done a wonderful job of sharing their standard of living with their children, but a miserable job of endowing those children with the skills they'll need to achieve that standard on their own."

Looked at from a slightly different perspective, the problem is that today's parents have worked too hard to keep their children happy. As a result, children grow up believing it's someone else's responsibility to take care of their needs and wants. Never having learned to accept responsibility for their own well-being, they go through life expecting other people to make them happy and blaming anything and everything that goes wrong on some*one* or some*thing* else. Unfortunately, as we all know, a person who fails to take full responsibility for his or her own happiness will never be fully happy. The paradox is this: The more parents take on responsibility for their children's happiness, the more they guarantee their children's eventual unhappiness.

In the first paragraph of the Declaration of Independence, it says ". . . that all men are created equal, that they are endowed by their Creator with certain unalienable Rights, that among these are Life, Liberty, and the pursuit of Happiness." Read it carefully. The Founding Fathers didn't say we have a right to *happiness*. They asserted our right to *pursue* happiness, and here's the root of the problem. When parents busy themselves in pursuit of happiness for their children, their children never learn to pursue it on their own. Yes, the pursuit is full of pitfalls and setbacks, but as bodybuilders say, "No pain, no gain." We should support children as they come to grips with the reality of frustration, but we must not protect them from it. For a child, the gain of learning to pursue happiness is measured in terms of self-esteem. The more we pursue that happiness for our children, therefore, the less chance they have of developing good self-esteem. There is no better reason than that for making sure your "parenting cabinet" is stocked with ample supplies of Vitamin N.

Tantrums

If common sense tells us that Vitamin N is essential to our children's well-being, then why do we work so hard to provide them with not only more in the way of material things than they need, but more than they're ever going to be able to attain for themselves as adults? Part of the problem, undoubtedly, has its roots in the "my children are going to have it better than I did" thinking that became increasingly prevalent following the hardships of the Great Depression and World War II. But it also has to do with the fact that many parents want to avoid the consequences of not giving in to their children's demands. I'm talking about tantrums of various sorts, from the two-year-old sort of rolling on the floor while screaming and frothing at the mouth to the sixteen-year-old sort of stomping and slamming doors while spewing forth a steady stream of verbal abuse. Quite a few parents are intimidated, even frightened, by tantrums. So, they give in. Some give in before the tantrum even starts. When they are asked, "why do you give in," they often answer, "Because it's easier to give in than it is to deal with the hassle."

That's true, but only in the short run. Giving in solves the immediate problem. It turns off the thrashing, the screaming, or whatever. In that sense, giving in is certainly "easier." Unfortunately, the more often parents give in to tantrums, the worse the tantrums become. Every time parents give in to a tantrum, they virtually guarantee the occurrence of at least fifty more.

If you give a child a choice between getting something the hard way and getting that same something in what looks like the easy way, the child will always choose the easy way. To a child, working and waiting for something, not to mention doing without, always looks like "the hard way." Wearing down a parent's resistance and resolve by screaming and stomping and arguing and cursing seems much easier. What the child doesn't know, and what many parents don't seem to realize, is that giving in to tantrums blocks the development of initiative, motivation, and resourcefulness. Without those survival tools, the child is destined to be a less successful, and therefore, less happy adult.

Guilt is another reason parents give in to tantrums. To parents who mistakenly believe that the measure of good parenting is a happy child, a tantrum says, "You aren't doing a good job." They seem to reason thusly: (a) Good parents raise happy children; (b) tantrums are a sign of unhappiness; therefore, (c) if our child throws a tantrum, we must have done something wrong. Thinking of this sort makes no sense, but it's very real and very common, nonetheless. Take, for example, a five-year-old who asks for a brownie thirty minutes before dinner. When his mother says "no," he begins whining and stomping around and saying absurd things like, "You never let me eat anything when I'm hungry!" Mom thinks the tantrum is evidence of a bad decision, one that may result in her child feeling insecure or unloved or—heaven forbid—resentful. So she hands over the brownie, knowing full well that, as a result, her child won't eat his supper. When, sure enough, he doesn't, she points out the connection between the brownie and his lack of appetite as if this information is going to render him more reasonable under similar, future circumstances. Mom's got a lot to learn.

All children can be counted on to throw tantrums of one sort or another. For one thing, children come into the world unequipped with any tolerance for frustration. For another, their original point of view is a self-centered (egocentric) one. Whatever they want, they believe they deserve. Part of our job as parents is to slowly but surely help our children dismantle that self-centeredness and replace it with a sense of social responsibility—a willingness to put personal concerns aside for the sake of family, friendship, and society. It could, in fact, be said that this is a parent's most important function. It is the essence of the socialization process, and that process involves a certain amount of discomfort. A child's natural reaction to that discomfort, to that disillusionment, is a tantrum. Looked at from this perspective, a tantrum is a child's way of divesting self-centeredness and growing up and into a more mature understanding of how the world works. It's essential, therefore, that parents learn how to say "no" to their children and say it with conviction.

I chuckle inside whenever I hear a parent complain that a certain child "can't take no for an answer." I'm amused because the comment always says more about the parent than it does the child. You see, a child who can't take "no" for an answer always has parents who can't really say it. It's not that he can't take "no," it's that he has no reason to believe it.

The fact that today's parents are not giving their children enough Vitamin N is not only weakening their children's character, but also has the potential of eroding the very foundation of our democratic society. After all, it was individual resourcefulness, perseverance, and a tolerance for frustration that made this country the greatest nation on earth.

For all these reasons, the next time you give your child a dose of Vitamin N, and he falls on the floor screaming, consider it a job well done!

Here's the Prescription!

You can start administering Vitamin N to your children in the following ways:

1. Turn their world right-side up by giving them all of what they truly need, but no more than 25 percent of what they simply want. I call this the "Principle of Benign Deprivation."

2. Don't do for your children what they are capable of doing for themselves. "You can do that on your own" pushes the growth of perseverance and self-sufficiency. When the child says, "I can't," don't argue. Just say, "Well, I *won't*." You'll be amazed at how creative and resourceful children can be under the right circumstances.

3. Don't always rescue them from failure and/or disappointment. Remember that falling on one's face can be an invaluable learning experience (see Point Three).

4. Remember that just because a child doesn't like something doesn't mean it shouldn't happen or exist. For example, the mere fact that a child doesn't want to be left with a babysitter doesn't mean he shouldn't be. For a child to grow up requires that his parents resist the temptation to constantly protect him from the discomfort of having to divest dependency.

5. Don't worry about treating children fairly. Remember that, to a child, "fair" means "me first," with the biggest and best of everything.

6. Remember that simply because you enjoy a good standard of living, doesn't mean you're obligated to share it in full with your children. Vitamin N gives children something to strive for along with the skills with which to strive.

7. Don't overdose your children emotionally by giving them too much attention or too much praise. If you pay too much attention to your children, they have no reason to pay attention to you (see Points One and Two).

Questions?

Q: Our three-year-old daughter throws a tantrum whenever she doesn't get her way. How should we handle them?

A: I'll answer your question by telling you a story about my daughter Amy: When she was two, and throughout the third year of her life, Amy was remarkably easy to get along with. Looking back, compared to most two-year-olds, she was relatively maintenance-free. If we told her to straighten her room, she straightened her room. Sometimes she straightened her room without even being asked. If she wanted something and we said "no," she shrugged it off without a whimper. She demanded very little time or attention from us and was quite adept at occupying herself for long periods of time.

Then, just about the time Willie and I were preparing to heave a sigh of relief and give thanks for this unexpected reprieve, the tantrums began. And did they ever! As though she was determined to make up for lost time, three-year-old Amy searched high and low for excuses to do the terrible-tantrum-thing. She screamed whenever we stopped her from doing what she wanted to do. She screamed whenever we refused to meet her demands, which became legion. She screamed whenever we assigned her a task, no matter how small. Sometimes she screamed for no apparent reason.

But screaming wasn't all she did. Amy began a tantrum by becoming rigid and then bouncing up and down on the balls of her feet while making a rapid, "Uh, uh, uh," sound that got progressively louder and longer until it became a full-blown wail: "Uuuuuuuuuuuuaaaaaaaaaaaaahhhhhhhhhhhhhhhhhhh!" By then, Amy was usually flapping her arms and running around in circles like a whirling dervish. At some point, she would collapse on the floor in a heap and begin thrashing about.

Having become desensitized to tantrums by Eric—whose tantrums, believe it or not, were worse than Amy's—Willie and I usually sat reading the paper or some such thing until the storm blew over. After several months, however, we noticed that despite our careless attitude toward Amy's tantrums, they were getting worse. We decided to take another approach.

One fairly peaceful afternoon, I took Amy aside for a talk. "Amy," I said, "you've been screaming a lot lately. So much, in fact, that mommy and daddy are going to give you a special place of your very own to scream in. We have lots of special places in the house. We have special places to sleep in, special places to eat in, and special places to go to the bathroom and take baths in. And now, you're going to have a special place to scream in! Come with me and I'll show you where it is."

I led her to the downstairs bathroom. Opening the door and ushering her inside, I continued: "This is it, Amy, your very own screaming place. And a fine screaming place it is, too. Why, just look! The walls are nice and close to make the screams louder, and there's soft carpet on the floor for you to roll around on. And if you scream so loud that you have to go to the bathroom, the toilet is right over here. And if you scream your throat dry, here's a sink and a cup for you to drink from.

"From now on, whenever you want to scream, just come in here and scream all you want. If you start to scream, but forget to come here, mommy and daddy will help you remember."

During my monologue, Amy did nothing but stand there with a "You must be crazy!" look on her face. Never one to pass up a challenge, it wasn't fifteen minutes before she was screaming and thrashing about something. I quickly said, "That's a very fine scream, Amy, but you must scream in your special place," and dragged her into the bathroom.

The first few times this happened, she would stop screaming, come back out, and begin screaming again. One of us would just as promptly put her back in the bathroom. Once she realized this was going to be standard operating procedure, the screams stopped almost as soon as the door closed. Nevertheless, she would remain in the bathroom pouting and scheming (or so I surmised) for several minutes. Then she'd emerge and, without as much as a glance in our direction, go to her room.

Within a couple of months, she had her tantrums under control. One morning, I passed by her room and heard what sounded like crying coming from inside. I opened the door.

"Are you all right?" I asked.

"Yes," she said, dry-eyed.

"Were you crying?"

"No. Bumpo was." (Bumpo was her teddy bear.)

"Oh. Where is Bumpo? I don't see him."

Amy walked over to her corner cabinet and opened the door. There sat Bumpo, looking rather forlorn.

"In *his* screaming place," she announced.

Q: The "Tantrum Place" idea sounds great for tantrums that take place at home. But what if our daughter has a tantrum in a store or some other public place?

A: First, don't try to talk her out of it. Second, don't try to ignore it, because you can't. Third, get her out of the public eye. As quickly as possible, take her either to a remote part of the store or outside and wait there until the tantrum runs its course. If she seems determined to keep it up, go home and use the "tantrum place." In the long run, it's worth the inconvenience.

Q: What should we say to our children when they point out, and correctly so, that all of their friends have a certain thing? If they don't have what their friends have, won't this hurt their self-esteem?

A: No, it won't hurt their self-esteem. Self-esteem is not a function of how many things we have, although we sometimes try to delude ourselves otherwise. It's a function of getting in touch with one's inner resources, the gifts that lie within. The more outward, material distractions there are in a child's life, the more likely it is the child will search in the wrong places for self-esteem.

When they were younger, one of our children's favorite

litanies was "But all my friends have one!" I never argued. Instead, I said, "I know. And I know how it feels to not have something your friends have. But your friends will share their good fortune with you, just as you will share what you have with them. That's what friends are for. In any case, you'll live." And you know what? They did!

Q: If I say "no" to my son and later realize I should have said "yes," should I change my mind and let him do or have what he wanted, or should I stick to my original decision?

A: It depends. If your son handled the "no" fairly well, and you said it only because of stresses that had nothing to do with him, then feel free to change your mind. On the other hand, if he threw a tantrum and/or needs more Vitamin N in his life anyway, then stick to your guns. Rest assured, it won't kill him or do him any psychological damage to live with parents who occasionally make irrational decisions. Besides, isn't life a bit irrational at times?

Q: Our thirteen year-old has reached the age where standard-brand clothing will no longer do. Like her friends, she wants clothes with designer labels. How can we get her to understand that cost and quality don't necessarily go together?

A: You can't, and trying will only make you blue in the face.

When Eric and Amy were into their teens, we solved this problem by opening personal checking accounts into which we deposited their monthly clothing and recreation allowances. When they ran out of money, their shopping and recreation for the month came to a halt. Through trial-and-error, they learned to budget, stretch their money, shop for bargains, and generally do more with less. Once they began earning their own money, our contribution went down and theirs went up. It was just another way of helping them out of our lives.

Q: I recently read an article on "the family bed." The author maintained that children, even older children, who sleep with their parents are more self-reliant, happy, and secure than children who do not. Should we bring our children, ages seven and four, into our bed?

A: Not unless you want two children who are less self-reliant and less secure, and happy only if they are sleeping with you. The claims of "family bed" advocates are completely bankrupt. There is not a shred of evidence to support them, but there is plenty with which to refute them.

The point of assigning a specific bedtime for children and having them sleep in their own beds, in their own rooms, is twofold. First, it gives parents much-needed time for themselves and one another. Second, bedtime is an exercise in separation and, therefore, independence. It is, in fact, the first of many such exercises to come, and how parents handle it sets an important and enduring precedent.

Separation involves a certain amount of anxiety for parents and children, especially young children. But the issue of separation, because it demands that children become less dependent and more self-sufficient, is inseparable from the task of growing up.

In his best-selling book, *The Road Less Traveled*, psychiatrist M. Scott Peck says that many people never learn to accept the inherent pain of living. When confronted with a problem, they either attempt an impatient, knee-jerk solution or try to ignore it altogether. Parents who spank children for crying at bedtime fall into the first category. Parents who let their children sleep with them fall into the second. Both are failing to deal with the issue.

In eighteen years of working with families, I've talked with many parents who slept with their children. But not once have I talked with a parent who was comfortable with the arrangement. Why, then, weren't these children sleeping alone? The usual answer: "Because so-and-so screams when we try to put him in his own bed." What so-and-so's parents don't realize is that the longer they avoid dealing with the issue of separation, the more anxiety it will arouse in so-and-so, and the more screams it will therefore provoke.

In Peck's terms, family sleeping is a way of avoiding a

problem in the hopes that somehow, someday, the problem will miraculously resolve itself. Unfortunately, life will probably deal a different hand to family sleepers.

The child whose parents avoid confronting the pain of separation never receives complete, implicit permission to separate from them. As the years go by, the parents' continued failure to resolve this fundamental issue becomes an obstacle to healthy growth and development. In my experience and, I daresay, the experience of most other clinicians, these children are generally excessively dependent, fearful, socially immature, and undisciplined.

At some point, nearly all young children cry at bedtime, and their cries make us want to draw them protectively closer. But protection of this nature is not always in a child's best interest. Children must learn to deal with separation; parents must show the way, and bedtime is a logical first place to begin the lessons. It's not as hard as it may sound. Establish a predictable bedtime and a routine to precede it. If the child cries, do not—as some pediatricians and child psychologists advise—let him "cry it out." Return to the bedroom at regular intervals to reassure him that you are still here, watching over him. If, along with your reassurances, the child hears a steadfast insistence that he stay in his bed, it won't be long before he accepts bedtime as a routine matter of fact.

Q: My eight-year-old daughter is afraid to try new things. She also becomes easily discouraged when her first attempt at something doesn't succeed. For example, if I try to encourage her to swim three laps of the pool instead of two, she'll say, "I can't." No matter how much I encourage or try to pump up her self-confidence, she won't make the attempt. If her piano teacher assigns her a difficult piece, she'll hardly try it before giving up. I can't understand why this otherwise capable child has such low self-esteem. How can I help her?

A: Your daughter's problem has less to do with self-esteem and more to do with the way you're responding to her frustrations. You're letting yourself get too emotionally involved in your daughter's performance, whether it be in swimming or piano or whatever.

Learning any new skill involves a certain amount of frustration. When your daughter encounters it, you go to her rescue. Although your intentions are good, you're actually preventing her from working through the frustration on her own, in her own way, and in her own time. Her stubborn refusal to heed your words of encouragement is a way of saying, "Back off, Mom." You see, when you get involved in these situations, your daughter has to deal with not only her frustrations, but yours as well. To her, your encouragement feels like pressure. So the more you encourage, the more she resists.

Let your daughter work these things out on her own. If she wants to talk to you about problems she's having learning a piano piece or swimming the length of the pool, listen to her but let her do most of the talking. When it's time for you to talk, say, "Learning new things takes a lot of effort and patience. Losing patience means it's time to set the thing aside for awhile and come back to it later." In other words, give her permission to be frustrated and even to "give up," at least temporarily.

If she still insists that she "can't," shrug your shoulders and say, "Well, then don't. If you think you've done your best and you're convinced you can't do it, then maybe you *should* give up. After all, if you've tried your best, giving up makes sense." Short and sweet. Then, walk away.

By not getting emotionally involved in her frustrations, you let her be completely responsible for her own feelings. My dad used to call it "stewing in one's own juices." When you stay out of it, you also give her freedom to try again, because now she can make that attempt on *her* terms rather than yours. Chances are, she will.

Q: Our daughter started kindergarten this year. Every evening, after supper, I sit with her at the kitchen table while she does her homework, which never amounts to much. Missy's problem is she doesn't make her numbers and letters well enough to suit herself and thinks her coloring is ugly. Consequently, she ends up doing everything over three or four times, when her first attempt was perfectly fine. The more I reassure, the madder she gets. At times, she's made statements such as "I'm dumb!" and "I can't do anything!" Her teacher sees none of this at school. How can I help her?

A: Let's keep things in their proper perspective: Missy is going through some major changes. She's in school for the first time; she's learning new skills; she's trying to please you; she's trying to please the teacher; she's trying to please herself; and, on top of all this, she has homework to do. Little wonder that she's feeling some pressure.

The way you manage this homework problem will be precedent-setting. In the final analysis, you want her to accept responsibility for her homework, set realistic goals for herself, and take pride in what she accomplishes. You don't want her to become a neurotic perfectionist at age five.

Two things are clear: First, you know she can do the work and do it well. Second, she doesn't get bent out of shape about her work in front of her teacher. Why? Because the teacher can't (and probably won't) give her as much attention as you can. Ah-ha! So now we know that the less attention Missy gets, the better her attitude toward herself and her work becomes. So stop giving her so much attention. Make three rules:

—Rule One: Missy does her homework in her room. No more kitchen table.

—Rule Two: If she wants help, she must ask for it. If you know she's capable of doing it on her own, tell her so in a supportive, encouraging way: "Oh, you can do that by yourself. You don't really need my help."

—Rule Three: She can only work on homework for thirty minutes. Set a timer. When it goes off, make her stop, whether she's finished or not. This will limit her obsessing and prevent homework from becoming a marathon.

If she complains of not being able to do this or that, just say, "I won't listen to things I know aren't true. I love you and trust you to do your best." Don't labor over this issue. The more you try to persuade her that she's capable, the more she'll complain.

Without intending to do so, Missy has manufactured this problem. There is, after all, no evidence whatsoever that it exists outside her imagination (or even outside of the kitchen). In effect, it's a soap opera, and she's the producer. When you stop being the audience, it will quickly go off the air.

Q: We have two boys, ages ten and seven. We've always done the same for both, thinking this was the way to prevent jealousy. It hasn't worked. They're constantly on the lookout for things one has or gets that the other doesn't. The situation is getting completely out-of-hand. What should we do?

A: If it's any consolation, the same plan has backfired for thousands of parents before you and will continue to backfire for thousands yet to come.

The solution? Stop treating them fairly. In the first place, your well-intentioned "fairness" is actually unfair, because no one will ever make any effort to treat them so fairly again. The more accustomed they get to the idea that "fair" is the normal way of the world, the ruder their awakening will eventually be. In the process of being fair, you've become a slave to their demands. They find your omissions, and you dutifully correct them. So, I ask you, who's running the show?

Q: So how do you propose I go about undoing five years of fairness?

A: Just tell them the game's over. Sit them down and read them your proclamation of independence: "Hear ye! Hear ye! Let it be henceforth known and proclaimed throughout the household that your parents are no longer going to be fair. Since it has become increasingly obvious to us that you are two different people, we are going to treat you—you guessed it—differently! If, for instance, we buy you (point dramatically at one of them) something, we may not buy you (point, with a flourish, at the other) anything at all. If we do something with or for you (point accusingly), we may not do anything with or for you (point menacingly). If that's not fair, so be it. If you don't like it—and you won't—that's life! Get the point?"

Now, the important stuff: You're in the habit of being fair and your boys are in the habit of expecting it. There's only one way to break a habit, and that's cold turkey. From now on, you and your husband should conspire to plan instances of unfairness. For example, take one son to the store and buy him a new pair of shoes. Several days later, take the other to the store and buy him a new sweatshirt. Plan things for them individually,

130

rather than collectively. It's the only way they're ever going to find out that unfair isn't terminal.

They won't like it. They will scream, rant, rave, act pitiful, blaspheme you, and that's just for starters. When they do, you will have the urge to sit them down and explain why you're doing what you're doing and how it's in their best interests, and blah, blah, blah. *Don't!* They won't agree with you, much less even listen. The harder you try to get them to "understand," the more they'll rant. Pretty soon you'll begin to feel that maybe you're doing the wrong thing and you'll try to be fair to make up for your awfulness and, *zap!*, you'll be right back where you started. Instead of entertaining their misery, just request that they take it to their rooms and vent it against their pillows and mattresses.

Q: Are there ever times when we should be fair?

A: If by what you mean, "Are there ever times when we should do the same thing for both of them?"—the answer is "Sure." I'm not suggesting that you never do the same thing for both of them or include them in the same activity. You wouldn't be a family any more if you did that.

Q: How long will it take before they adjust to our unfairness?

A: I'd say it will take three to six months for the screaming to stop, another three to six years for them to get completely used to the idea, and adulthood before they understand why you did it and forgive you.

Q: At least ten times a day, every day, my four-year-old daughter asks me if I love her. I always tell her I love her very much and always will. Several months ago, when this first started, I thought it was a phase that would pass quickly. Instead of tapering off, however, it's gotten steadily worse. I can't figure out what might have caused her to become so insecure. What would you advise?

A: I'd advise that you help your daughter stop asking the question so much.

In the first place, asking "Do you love me?" ten times a day doesn't mean your daughter is insecure. She's probably just trying to figure out what "love" means and how long it lasts. Repetition is one way children answer questions of this sort for themselves.

Illustration: If you capture a six-month-old's interest by moving a brightly colored object through her field of vision, and then hide it behind your back, she won't come in search of it. In her mind, the object no longer exists. Several months later, she'll respond to the same tease by crawling behind you to find it. Around eight months of age, an infant realizes that objects don't cease to exist when they're out of sight.

I've watched a ten-month-old amuse himself by placing a block inside a kitchen pot, putting the lid on the pot, and then immediately taking it off to rediscover the "lost" block. Like a scientist, he repeated this simple experiment over and over again until he had proven to himself that the block was forever.

In a like manner, your daughter is trying to establish the identity and permanence of an intangible concept—an invisible idea—by taking the lid off the question, "Do you love me?" time and time again.

The problem isn't the question. It's that adults are generally insecure about their ability to raise children and tend, therefore, to look for and seize upon every possible indication that something is terribly wrong. We overanalyze and misinterpret events, we blow the significance of things completely out of proportion, we misplace common sense and replace it with nonsense.

At some point, your daughter probably began to sense that the question made you feel somewhat uncomfortable. Needing to understand why mommy got so flustered, she began asking the question more and more often. The more she asked, the more flustered you became, the more she asked, and so on.

The two of you are riding the same merry-go-round. You don't know how to stop getting flustered, and she doesn't know how to stop asking the question. She can't help you. So, as I said to begin with, you've got to help her.

Find a peaceful, relaxed time for the two of you to sit down and talk. Tell her that "I love you" is like a piece of candy people surprise one another with, and that you would like to begin surprising her with it, too. Help her understand that you can't surprise her as long as she asks the question.

Then, the next time she asks, say something like, "Oh-oh, now it's not a surprise."

Meanwhile, make it a point to call her over to you several times a day to play "Guess What."

"Guess what?"

"What?"

"I love you."

Personally, I can't think of a nicer surprise.

Q: Is it okay to let an adult child live at home? If so, what understandings should exist between the parents and the child?

A: Valid reasons for letting a grown child come home to nest include such things as divorce, job loss, and prolonged illness. Stressful circumstances such as these might temporarily interfere with the young person's ability to be self-supporting, in which case equally temporary parental help might be necessary.

"Nesting" is also perfectly acceptable during major, but not necessarily stressful, transitions in the child's life. These would include the time between college graduation or the end of military service and a job. If living at home for a few months prior to getting married would help the young person build a nest egg, that's fine too.

Whatever the circumstances, the arrangement should not be "open ended." Parents and child should establish goals, a specific plan of action, and time frames for reaching those goals. For example, the agreement might stipulate that the young person will be out of the house in six months. The first month will be spent finding a job, the second and third paying off debts, the fourth and fifth building a financial cushion, and the sixth finding an affordable place to live.

During this period of dependency, the young person should be required to make some form of contribution to the household. If unable to contribute financially, he or she should perform services around the home which function as payment.

133

Once the young person has income, a sliding scale of financial reimbursement can be worked out. He should, in other words, "earn his keep."

Q: How much control should parents exercise over an adult child who lives at home?

A: No more than they would exercise over any other temporary boarder. This arrangement involves three adults, not two adults and one child. The young person should be treated as an adult and be expected to act as such. Likewise, the parents should act as adults, not parents. This means, for example, that the parents should set no specific restrictions on the young person's comings and goings. It also means that the young person should come and go with due respect for the parents' lifestyle and values.

Q: What if the young person violates the agreement or behaves in a manner that's annoying or offensive to the parents?

A: The parents shouldn't lecture or punish the young person for behavior they don't like, but should express their concerns in a straightforward manner. Violations of the agreement should be openly discussed, the goal being to reach understanding as to why the violation occurred and prevent a repeat performance. Perhaps the violation was the result of a misunderstanding, or perhaps the agreement was unrealistic to begin with and needs to be modified. If conflict continues between parents and child, then family counseling is the next step.

Q: What if the agreed-upon time for leaving comes and the young person isn't financially able to leave?

A: Inventory what went wrong and why. Set new goals based on the mistakes and miscalculations that were made and try again. If the young person fails a second time to emancipate on schedule, there may be more going on than meets the eye. At that point, it may be appropriate to explore the issues and problems with a family counselor.

POINT
FIVE

Toys
and Play:
The Right Stuff

I remember being five years old. My life was chock-full of
stone walls and trees to climb, lizards to catch, nooks and
crannies to explore, and parks and empty lots in which to play. I
had no television during those early years—didn't even know it
existed—and very few store-bought toys. But my imagination
had wings and fly I did, to whatever place and in whatever
pretend-person I pleased.

We lived for a time in a southern coastal city, and I spent
many an afternoon in a park down by the waterfront, watching
the big ships and dreaming of faraway places like London,
where the Queen lived, and Africa, where Tarzan swung
through the trees with the apes.

Every night, either my mother or my grandmother would
read to me from children's classics like Kipling's *Just So Stories, The Wind in the Willows,* or Thurber's *Thirteen Clocks.*
Because my mother worked a part-time job in addition to
attending college, I went to a preschool where we played games
and painted pictures with our fingers and made castles out of
empty oatmeal boxes and soldiers out of clothespins (the kind
with no springs). Mom used to tell me we were "dirt poor," but

looking back, the standard of *my* living was high. It was a special time, but not out of the ordinary, because that's what childhood was all about way back then.

But time has taken its toll on childhood. So much so that, at times, I fear we may be poised on the brink of childhood's end. Not the final apocalyptic end of children, mind you, but the loss of what being a child once was and still should (and can) be all about.

Today, instead of sending children outdoors to play, we let them sit in front of television sets for thousands of hours during their formative years, staring at a constantly blinking, tasteless, odor-free, hands-off, counterfeit of the real world. Meanwhile, their imaginations atrophy from disuse, along with their initiative, their curiosity, their resourcefulness, and also their creativity.

Today, instead of providing children with ample opportunity and the raw materials with which to find and create handmade playthings, we overdose them with mass-produced toys that stimulate relatively little imaginative thought—toys that are nothing more than what the labels on their boxes say they are.

Today, instead of reading to children and letting time and teachers do the rest, we push letters and numbers at preschoolers, completely disregarding the fact that early childhood has nothing to do with letters and numbers and everything to do with play. We have, in fact, little respect for the enormous contribution play makes to healthy growth and development. "He's just playing," we're apt to say, when "just playing" is the very essence of childhood.

Before going any further, I'm going to take you on a guided tour of a typical child's life, circa 1989. Let's begin in his/her room, otherwise known as Toytown. There are toys strewn all over the floor, wedged under the bed, stuffed in the cabinets, packed onto the shelves, crammed in the closet, and even dangling from the ceiling. But wait! There's more to come! Downstairs, there are toys decorating the floor in the living room and the den. There are more lining the wall of the garage, and still more outside, rusting in the yard. If this child is not yet of school age, he/she probably attends a preschool program where most of the day is spent playing with an assortment of brightly colored plastic toys, coloring mimeographed pictures, and learning to recite and write the ABC's. How exciting! If this child is of school age, then it's likely that several afternoons through the week are taken up with such absolutely essential things as soccer practice, piano lessons, and classes in social etiquette.

And yet, in the midst of all of these things and all of these activities, we are probably going to find a child who makes one complaint more than any other—namely, "I'm bored!" In fact, if I were to give a name to the present generation of children, it would be the "I've Got Nuthin' to Do" generation. That is, after all, their favorite litany.

When I was five, I had five toys. They were a set of Lincoln Logs, a set of Tinker Toys, an electric train that ran on twelve feet of circular track, a set of lead cavalry and foot soldiers, and a "Hopalong Cassidy" pearl-handled cap pistol with black leather holster. With the exception of my toy gun, which I was allowed to wear as often as I wanted, my mother kept those toys in a box on the upper shelf of her closet. She called them "Rainy-Day Things." If the weather permitted, she expected me to be outside. That box came down only if the weather was inclement or night had fallen early. But I was never bored. I was *never* at a loss for something to do. And if I had complained of being bored, I'm certain my mother would have found something to occupy my time, but it probably wouldn't have been amusing.

How can it be that today's children, for whom parents provide so much in the ways of things and activities, are so constantly bored? Actually, the question answers itself. Today's children are bored precisely *because* parents provide them with so many things and activities.

Too many toys overwhelm a child's ability to make creative decisions. He can't decide what to do next because the clutter presents too many options. So, he retreats from the chaos, saying, "I've got nuthin' to do." At first, his parents are annoyed by his expressions of helplessness. Eventually, however, they become fed up with his whining and complaining and buy him a new toy. It works! He stops complaining! For a while, that is. As quickly as his interest in the new toy wanes, the child begins again to whine about being bored. What his parents are slow to realize is that instead of solving the child's boredom, the new toy only makes it worse. In the long run, it only adds to the clutter and strengthens his growing addiction to acquired things.

The child's boredom also has a lot to do with the *kinds* of toys his parents buy. In most cases, today's toys are one-dimensional—a truck, a boat, a this or a that. The singular nature of most mass-produced playthings limits a child's ability to express imagination and creativity, making boredom that much more likely.

What it boils down to is that, with the best of intentions, we've successfully prevented today's children from getting in touch with the "magical make-do" of childhood. When I was a child, play was largely a matter of make-do. For instance, if "pirates" was the game of the day, I'd borrow one of my mother's brightly colored scarfs for a sash and her black galoshes for ten-league boots. A stick became my broadsword. Mom helped me make a hat by folding a sheet of newspaper. A few pieces of her costume jewelry completed the disguise. Looking at myself in the mirror, I was Captain Blood! Together, my mates and I sailed the seven backyards in search of milk and cookies. Oh, what fun!

For the most part, today's children don't know how to make-do. Why? Because they've never had to. Too much has been done for them, too much given to them. Their teachers (who should know) tell me that instead of inventing games, today's children tend to mimic characters and situations from popular television programs. (That eliminates "pirates" from the running.) Props aren't improvised, they're purchased at a toy store. How boring! How sad.

Through the magic of making-do, children exercise imagination, initiative, creativity, intelligence, resourcefulness, and self-reliance. In the process, they practice discovery and invention, which are the basics of science. Making-do is not only the essence of truly creative play, which is, in turn, the essence of childhood, it's also the story of the advancement of the human race. Throughout the parade of history, the art of making-do has been significant to nearly every important invention and nearly every famous discovery. The child who discovers the magic of make-do is on the road to success and self-esteem!

Who knows, that same child might be our next Marie Curie, Louis Pasteur, Jonas Salk, Ferdinand Magellan, Thomas Edison, Alexander Graham Bell . . . who knows?

Charlie's Magic Make-Do Marker

Somewhere, in a present place and a present time, there lives a five-year-old boy named Charlie. One day, Charlie's parents hear strange noises coming from his room—"Sssssssszzzzzooooommmmmmmmm! POW! POW! POW! POW! Nnnnneeeeeyyyooow!"

Charlie's parents tiptoe quietly down the hall to check things out. As they get closer, the sounds get louder. Quietly, they crack Charlie's door just enough to see without being seen. Charlie is running excitedly around his room, tracing sweeping arcs in the air with an empty felt-tip-marker-turned-rocketship he managed to rescue from the trash. Suddenly, Charlie stops. The sound becomes a high-pitched whine as the "spaceship" begins its vertical descent to the surface of "Planet Chest-of-Drawers." It lands and for a moment, nothing moves. Then, "Click, click, click," says Charlie, and his parents can almost see the hatch of the spaceship open and its alien commander emerge.

Instantly, the magic marker becomes the alien and begins to lumber ominously across the surface of the planet, looking for something good to eat. The alien doesn't get very far when suddenly, from behind a wad of rolled-up underwear, there jumps a plastic Indian, with bow drawn. "Whoooooosssshh!" the Indian lets fly an arrow at the alien. As the intruder moves to defend itself, the magic marker becomes a ray gun, which it begins firing at the Indian, making a rapid "shhooooommmm-shooooommm!" sound. For the next three or four minutes, the battle rages. Finally, sensing the advantage, the Indian emerges from behind the shelter of his underwear rocks, shouts a ferocious war cry, and charges at the startled alien. Realizing that death rays are no match for a crazed Indian with bow-and-arrow, the alien beats a hasty retreat and blasts off in search of a more hospitable planet.

Closing Charlie's door, his parents tiptoe back to the living room. "Well," says Charlie's father, "now we know what to get Charlie for Christmas."

"We certainly do," says Charlie's mother, and together they chorus, "A rocket ship!"

And so, on Christmas morning, Charlie wakes up to find a huge box under the tree labeled "To Charlie from Santa." Inside, he finds a replica of the space shuttle, complete with cargo hatch, a command module with seating for seven astronauts, and retractable landing gear. Inside the box, Charlie finds a plastic dropcloth printed to look like the surface of the moon. The box itself, when folded in a certain manner, makes a ridge of moon-mountains. Charlie is absolutely consumed with joy! But the spaceship isn't all Charlie gets on Christmas morning. There's also a battery-operated car he can steer by remote control. There's a slot-car racing set. There's a man on a motorcycle that winds up and leaps from ramp to ramp. Finally, there's a suitcase that opens to reveal a miniature city and comes complete with tiny cars to drive around the city's streets. Oh, joy! Charlie really rakes it in on Christmas morning!

Three weeks later, Charlie's mother is in the kitchen fixing dinner when Charlie drags in, looking dejected. His mother asks, "Charlie? What's the matter with you?" Charlie scuffs the floor with his toe and whines, "I've got nuthin' to do."

Charlie's mother goes into cerebral meltdown. She turns on him and shrieks, "What do you mean, telling me you've got nothing to do!? You've got a new space shuttle, a remote-controlled car, a man on a motorcycle, and a city in a suitcase, not to mention all the other toys you have back in your room from birthdays and Christmases past! *How dare you tell me you've got nothing to do!?*"

What Charlie's mother fails to realize is that Charlie is telling the truth. He really doesn't have anything to do. He's done everything that can be done with a space shuttle, a remote control car, a man on a motorcycle, and a city in a suitcase. What Charlie really needed on Christmas morning were toys he could *do* things with, rather than toys that are nice to look at, cost a lot of money, and perform at the flip of a switch. You see, the difference between Charlie's marvelous magic marker and a seventy-five dollar plastic replica of the space shuttle is that the magic marker was anything Charlie wanted it to be. In the span of a mere few minutes, it was a spaceship, an alien, and a ray gun. And all Charlie did to effect these transformations was zap it with the alchemy of his imagination. But no matter how much Charlie imagines his space shuttle to be something else, it remains a space shuttle, forever and ever, Amen. Within three weeks, Charlie exhausted all of the creative potential of not only the space shuttle, but also the remote-controlled car, the man on the motorcycle, and the city in the suitcase. And so, three weeks after Christmas, Charlie truly has nothing to do.

Transformations

Like Charlie's empty felt-tip marker, all truly creative toys have one characteristic in common: They encourage and enable children to perform what are called "transformations." A child performs a transformation whenever he uses something, any-thing, to represent something else. For instance, when a child takes a pinecone and sets it upright on the ground and calls it a tree, that's a transformation. Transformations are the essence of fantasy, which is, in turn, the essence of play. In a child's hands, an empty box becomes a boat, a car, a table, or anything else he *wills* it to be. A child can also transform himself into anyone he wants to be—Tarzan, Jane, or the neighborhood grocer. If a toy aids a child in making transformations, then it is well-worth the money spent on it, not to mention the time the child spends playing with it.

Toys which encourage transformations include creative materials such as clay, fingerpaints, and crayons. Inside, there's the everyday household stuff of empty oatmeal cartons, Popsicle sticks, spoons, shoeboxes, empty spools of thread, straws, paper bags, buttons, pots and pans, and empty toilet paper rolls. And don't forget how much fun children have turning large appliance cartons into houses! Outside, there are leaves, sticks, pinecones, rocks, and mud, glorious mud! The list goes on and on, limited only by the limits of the child's virtually limitless imagination.

As a child, one of my favorite toys was a Quaker Oatmeal box. I could make it into just about anything I wanted. I'd turn it upside down, thread a neck-band of string through two holes punched in the side and it became a "drum" which I played with wooden spoons. Or, I'd cut rectangular notches in the top and a drawbridge in the side and it became a castle. Or, I'd tape a brim to it and it became a top hat. How much did these toys cost? The price of oatmeal. How much did I gain from them? An incredible amount. After all, I'd made them with my own hands.

While your children are young, show them how to use things like pots and pans, empty boxes, pipe cleaners, and other odds-and-ends to make their own toys. Once you show a child what can be done with a box, some tape, a few sheets of construction paper, and a pair of scissors, there'll be no stopping him! A child who makes his own playthings is not only learning how to entertain himself, but is also exercising independence, self-sufficiency, initiative, resourcefulness, eye-hand coordination, intelligence, imagination, achievement motivation, creativity, and, therefore, self-esteem. What more could a parent want? There are few investments of a parent's time and energy that will pay off better than this one.

Buying Worthwhile Toys

Realizing that the average American child is a toy addict, many toy companies make toys with purposefully (and profitably) short life spans. After all, why make toys that last when the average child is more concerned with *getting* than with the quality of what's gotten?

When buying toys for children, consider first the fact that children are inquisitive. The first question that pops into their minds when they're given something is, "How does it work?" In most cases, you find out how something works by taking it apart. Unfortunately, most toys are not made to be taken apart. If you try, they will break.

ZENITH'S ANIMATED, INTER-
ACTIVE, MICROCHIP- DRIVEN
BEAR WITH VOICE, EYE, MOUTH
AND PAW MOVEMENTS
SYNCHRONIZED TO A SET OF
VIDEOTAPE PRODUCTIONS OF
"AESOP'S FABLES."

ZENITH'S HANDCRAFTED
ITALIAN TEAK BUILDING-
BLOCK SET WITH TINY FIG-
URES OF THE COMPLETE CAST
OF THE "CIRQUE DU SOLEIL"...
... ZENITH'S ERGONOMICALLY
CORRECT, MONO-FORK, FRONT-
SUSPENSION TRICYCLE....

© 1988 Universal Press Syndicate

ZENITH'S NATURAL FIBER
TYRANNOSAURUS PUPPET THAT
SINGS THE FRENCH ALPHABET
TO THE TUNE OF "OLD MAC DON-
ALD"...ZENITH'S $300 LIBRARY
OF POP-UP BOOKS FROM THE
MUSEUM OF MODERN ART....

ZENITH'S FAVORITE TOY : AN
EMPTY TOILET PAPER TUBE.

Consider also that most toys are designed to attract the child's attention and curiosity, but not to hold his or her interest. This obviously profitable marketing philosophy is to blame for the fact that children lose interest in most toys within a few weeks, if not days.

Not all toy companies are into making schlock, but many are. So, how are parents to know whether the toys they are buying their children are good investments? In addition to being safe, a good toy embodies four qualities:

—First, it presents a wide range of creative possibilities. It is capable of being many things, as defined by the child's imagination, rather than one thing, as defined by the manufacturer. In other words, it enables transformations.

—Second, it encourages manipulation. It can be taken apart and put together in various ways. Toys of this kind hold a child's interest because they stimulate creative behavior.

—Third, it's age-appropriate. You don't give a rubber duck to a ten-year-old any more than you give an electric train to a two-year-old. Most manufacturers publish the age range of a toy on its box. While not always entirely accurate, these give a fairly good idea of whether the toy and the child will "match."

—Fourth, it's durable. It will withstand lots of abuse.

A toy that rates high in all four areas possesses excellent "play value." When parents ask me for examples of manufactured toys high in play value, the first that come to mind are the construction sets manufactured by Lego. In my estimation, these are the only toy systems that score a perfect "10" along all four of the above dimensions. Coming in a close second are building sets like Lincoln Logs, Tinker Toys, and Erector Sets. Art materials—clay, finger paints, construction paper, crayons, scissors—should be staples in every child's life.

By way of dolls, the new generation of cuddly, so-called "adoption dolls" enable children to explore parental feelings and act out parental behavior. They're far more imaginative and creative than dolls that walk, talk, drink from a bottle, and wet their pants.

While we're on the subject of dolls, I should mention how important it is that parents not limit children to toys traditionally considered appropriate to only one gender. Dolls and stuffed animals are just as appropriate for boys as they are for girls. If a boy wants to play with dolls, buy him dolls! If a girl wants to play baseball, buy her a bat and a ball! The freer children are to explore the possibilities of life, the better choice-makers whey will become.

Surprisingly, most high-priced "educational" toys rate low

on the "play value" scale. They are typically one-dimensional and challenge a child's imagination and intellect for a relatively short period of time. Educational toys appeal primarily to parents, who mistakenly think that toys of this type will speed their children's development or get them ready for school more rapidly. For the most part, however, their educational value is shallow, contrived, and either irrelevant to a child's development, or a poor substitute for cheaper, yet more interesting, materials and activities.

Notice that the toys mentioned above as being high in "play-value" have been on the market for thirty years or more. In addition to those already mentioned, toys that fit this criterion include blocks, electric trains (the child can use Legos and Lincoln Logs to make the train station and other buildings, Tinker Toys to make bridges and tunnels, etc.), Matchbox cars, small plastic figures (a bag of plastic army men or cowboys and Indians), dolls, dollhouses (the child can be taught to make furniture out of construction paper), cap pistols, and marbles. For the older child, purchase toys which can form the nucleus of a hobby, such as chemistry sets, telescopes and microscopes, rock-collecting sets, models, and the like. A child will get a lot more mileage out of a handful of old-fashioned toys than he/she will out of all the new-fangled junk in the world!

Less Is More

Several years ago, a couple consulted me concerning their almost three-year-old daughter. Most of the problems they described were typical of this age child, but one was especially intriguing.

"Molly won't let us out of her sight," they said. "In addition to following us wherever we go in the house, she's constantly asking us to play with her and whining if we can't. Neither of us minds playing with her some, but we feel that with all the toys she has, she ought to have no trouble entertaining herself."

My ears perked up. "How many toys does she have?" I asked. "And what kind are they?"

"She's got so many toys you can hardly walk into her room without stepping on one," said her father. "As to the kinds of toys she has, they're mostly the ones you see advertised on television, I guess."

That was all I needed to hear to know what the problem was.

First, I helped Molly's parents rate the play value of Molly's toys on a scale of one to ten. Those with ratings of less than seven were boxed and given to charity. Not surprisingly, that reduced the pile by nine-tenths. Those that remained included soft, gimmick-free dolls, some stuffed animals, a set of blocks, and a dollhouse.

Next, Molly's parents went toy shopping. Instead of the junk that constitutes most of the toys advertised on television, they bought a few toys that measured up to the criteria set forth earlier in this chapter.

To create a household environment that encouraged exploration, Molly's parents childproofed their home. They put up anything that was potentially dangerous as well as anything that couldn't be easily replaced if broken. This insured that Molly would be able to roam through most of the house without needing much supervision. Childproofing also minimized the number of times Molly had to hear the word "no," making obedience more likely.

Molly's parents also put safety latches on all the kitchen cabinets but one, which became "Molly's cabinet." Her parents stocked this secret place with empty oatmeal boxes, empty spools, old pots and pans, boxes of all sorts and sizes, and other safe household items that might otherwise have been discarded. Here was a place where Molly could come and rummage to her heart's content.

Last, but not least, Molly's parents went to an appliance store and obtained a large, sturdy box into which they cut windows and a door. A small chair went inside, along with a few dolls and other "housekeeping" items. Just the place for hours of imaginative play.

I saw Molly's parents several weeks later. Sure enough, Molly was entertaining herself much better than before and demanding far less of her parents' attention. "She seems," said her mother, "bright and happy again."

Molly's story isn't unique. In the last ten years, I've made the same basic set of recommendations to at least twenty parents. Of those, perhaps ten have had the gumption to follow through. The experiment has yet to fail. Every parent has reported the same basic results: The fewer the toys and the more space the child has in which to explore and create, the more successful the child is at occupying his/her time. And the more success the child experiences at what comes more naturally than anything else—play—the happier the child. These success stories simply go to show that sometimes, less is more.

Play-Fullness

The story of Molly underscores how important play is to healthy development.

First, play exercises the skills a child needs in order to become a fully competent individual. Play is a multi-dimensional experience, involving nearly all of a child's perceptual, motor, sensory, and cognitive equipment. It is a total-learning experience, unlike any other. Play is the catalyst, as well as the medium, of growth during early and middle childhood.

Second, a number of recent studies have demonstrated how important sufficient, unstructured playtime during early childhood is to the development of a well-rounded personality and healthy social skills. Children who are deprived of imaginative playtime are more likely to become either overly aggressive or depressed.

Third, play provides a nonthreatening context within which a child can explore and begin to understand the adult world. It is through fantasy play that children come to understand and work through things that might otherwise remain confusing— things like divorce, parental anger, death, and so on.

Fourth, play helps children relieve stress and develop a sense of humor. Along these same lines, play helps children grow up to become adults who are capable of having fun.

Play is also a vehicle for significant learning, especially that of learning how to learn. Through play, children ask questions, explore their environments, learn essential problem-solving skills, practice social roles, and—in general—strengthen all the faculties that will enable them to realize their potential.

Unfortunately, over the last thirty or forty years, we have managed to place a number of obstacles in the path of the young child's innate desire to express imagination and growth through play. We have inundated young children with toys that smother their powers of creativity. We have let them sit in front of television sets for hours upon hours while their imaginations atrophy from disuse. Instead of reading to children and letting time and the schools do the rest, we push flash cards and letters and numbers at preschool children, having lost sight of the fact that those activities are completely irrelevant to healthy growth and development.

The trend in recent years has been toward structuring the young child's time with organized sports, music lessons, classes in etiquette, early academic instruction, and so on. We mistakenly believe that these things are more "meaningful" than play, when exactly the opposite is true. Furthermore, because so much has been planned and done for them, many of today's children have forgotten how to plan and do for themselves.

Give the Kids Their Games Back

One of the most disturbing aspects of the after-school activities craze is the trend toward enrolling children, at younger and younger ages, in organized sports programs. In my hometown, for example, children as young as five are participating in "tee-ball," soccer, and competitive swimming. These programs are absolutely irrelevant to the developmental needs—social, physical, or otherwise—of young children. Moreover, they can actually be detrimental, especially during middle childhood (ages six to ten).

The psychology of the young school-age child can be summarized in two words: acceptance and achievement. Self-esteem hinges on how successful he is at creating a secure place for himself among his peers and at establishing and attaining specific goals of excellence.

Organized sports would seem to be an ideal complement to

the needs of children this age—the perfect medium in which to nurture both the inner and outer self. Not so. The primary problem is adult involvement. Adults organize these programs, adults raise the money to fund them, adults draw up the playing schedule, adults pick the teams, coach them, referee them, decide who plays and who doesn't, give out awards, and make up the biggest share of the audience.

But it doesn't stop there. Not only do adults play too prominent a role in planning and organizing these events, they also take it upon themselves to mediate such things as which children acquire what status within the peer group, how conflict between children is resolved, and so on.

Adults have absolutely no business being that involved in the play of children. Their presence is a complicating factor that prevents the children from learning to negotiate social issues on their own. All too often, instead of being activities for children, these events become theaters where youngsters are manipulated for the gratification of adults.

The fact that these sports are competitive is not, in and of itself, disturbing. A child this age needs and, if left to his own devices, will seek out appropriate competitive experiences. What *is* disturbing is that the children, because adults are so entangled in the proceedings, no longer play for fun, but to obtain adult approval. They are not really *playing* at all. They are *working*, performing for an adult audience.

The difference between competitive play and competitive work can be measured in terms of emotional outcome. When children band together to play a sandlot game, one team wins and one team loses, but everyone usually manages to leave the field feeling okay. When adults direct children in an organized sports event, the children on the losing team often end up feeling angry, dejected, frustrated, ashamed, and/or depressed. This isn't play. This is serious business, and the stakes are high. Too high.

In this context, the child-athlete's sense of achievement and self-esteem become defined in terms of winning and losing. Process and participation take a backseat to outcome, which isn't what childhood is all about. Everyone suffers, but the biggest losers are the children who don't get to play because they aren't "good" enough.

The basic problem—one that isn't limited to this issue—is the tendency of adults to act as though children will botch the job of growing up unless we engineer the process for them. The exact opposite is true. When we place ourselves *between* the child and the task of growing up, we are no longer in a helpful position. We are interfering and the child is ultimately less capable of dealing with life in the raw.

When he was about ten years old, Eric became interested in soccer and joined one of the teams in the neighborhood league. A proud father, I started attending the games. The stands were always packed with parents, many of them howling at the children to hustle more, be more aggressive, and so on. If they weren't howling at the players, they were howling at the referee. The coach paced the sidelines, looking very busy and very serious.

At the ends of these games, while mingling with the players and their parents, I frequently overheard comments like "If you're not going to hustle, then you shouldn't play" and "If you had been paying attention, that shot wouldn't have gotten by you." I was relieved when Eric told me he wanted to quit.

Several months later, Willie and I were at a local jogging track where a pee-wee football team was holding practice. When our run was over, we rested on the hill overlooking the field. By this time, practice had ended and all the little players in their pads and helmets were standing in a line at the end zone. We watched in growing amazement as the head coach strutted up and down in front of the boys, none of them older than nine, bellowing at them for being such "sissies."

"You're all a bunch of wimps and sissies!" He yelled. "You hit like a bunch of girls! Are you girls? You, Waldorf, are you a girl? Answer me, Waldorf! Are you a girl? No? Well then, what's the matter with you out there? Are you afraid you might get hurt? Don't start crying, Waldorf, 'cause I've got no sympathy for that kind of sissy stuff."

On and on he went as my blood pressure rose along with my sense of outrage. Willie prevented me from confronting him by pointing out that he was twice my size and obviously mean enough not to be impressed by my opinion of his vile harangue. In fact, he'd have probably welcomed the opportunity to demonstrate to the team how a "real" man handled conflict.

When I was a kid, sports was one of the most important things in my life. Along with the other boys in my suburban Chicago neighborhood, I played football in the fall, basketball in the winter, and baseball through the glory days of spring and summer. Our games were all pick-up games played on fields at the local school or the park. We got there on our bicycles. There were hardly ever enough players to make up two bona fide teams, so we modified the rules to suit the situation.

There were never any adults at our games. We were the players, the coaches, and the referees. We yelled at one another to hustle, we praised and criticized one another's play, we razzed one another. Despite all this, there were rarely hard feelings. It was all part of the game, and since the game was exclusively ours, we could do with it as we pleased. In the process, we learned how to subordinate our own desires to the best interest of the group, how to be good winners and good losers, how to resolve conflict, and how to begin running our own lives.

Little League Baseball was the only organized sport available outside of school sports, which didn't start until the seventh grade. Through our early teenage years, my buddies and I watched as the organized sports programs grew and began taking over the hallowed ground of our playing fields. The turning point for us came the day we were politely but firmly told to vacate a field we were playing on because a Little League team needed it for practice.

Some twenty-eight years later, I'm aware that children rarely play pick-up games anymore. Somewhere along the line, someone got the brilliant idea that sports would be more of a meaningful learning experience for children if the games were managed by adults. The adults could see to it that rules were followed, that play was fair, that the children's skills improved through proper coaching, that conflicts were resolved properly and so on.

The end result of all this well-intentioned meddling is that children don't have the opportunity to discover and work these issues out on their own. In addition, there's a tense and unhealthy air of professionalism that pervades organized children's sports programs. It's all too obvious that the children are on the field not to have fun, but to perform for adults who are all too eager to have their egos stroked.

And so, I voice my objections. And people respond by saying things like, "I know, I know, but John, sports are so competitive these days that if you don't start the kids out young, they won't be able to make the teams when they get to high school."

Hogwash! The same lame argument is used to justify pushing reading skills at preschool children. Studies show that the earlier you push reading at children, the less joy they bring to the task and the less successful they ultimately are. I suspect the same may be true of organized children's sports. And let's face it, joy—not parental pressure—is the essence of success, whether that success is in the classroom or on the athletic field.

I say let the kids have their games back.

Questions?

Q: *My best friend refuses to buy her children what she calls "war toys"—toy guns, army paraphernalia, super-hero action figures, and the like. She says they reinforce the notion that force is an acceptable way of resolving conflict. I'm undecided. What do you think?*

A: I can certainly appreciate your friend's point of view, but I don't think war toys have quite the impact on children she says they do. Unquestionably, if there were no such thing as war, there would be no war toys, but I doubt the reverse is true. Children have been playing with war toys and at war games for as long as man has waged war on himself. Nevertheless, there is no reason to believe that playing at war encourages actual aggressive behavior.

Children play at all manner of adult vocations and recreations. In fact, once children find out that adults do thus-and-such, they seek to understand that aspect of the grown-up world by playing at it. But a child's play does not determine a child's values. Children who play "married" and end up getting a pretend divorce are only trying to understand, through enactment, why grown-ups get divorced. Those same children aren't more likely, as adults, to think that divorce is the way to solve marital problems.

The quality and quantity of toys parents buy children certainly do have a significant effect on their development. As I've already said, too many toys of the wrong type can actually have a deprivational effect on the development of imagination, creativity, initiative, resourcefulness, and so on. But a child's value structure, his concept of right and wrong, is determined primarily through interaction with his parents, *not* through interaction with toys.

The same is true of war toys and war games. They are tools, not of menace, but understanding. In and of themselves, they are harmless. A child who plays at games like "war" and "cops and robbers" may even come to better grips with the reality of violence than a child who does not. A child who grows up in a climate of violence, however, is altogether a different story.

For the most part, I don't like war toys for the same reason I don't like the majority of toys in today's marketplace: They're too literal and therefore require/stimulate little imagination. A toy gun made out of Legos or a stick is far superior to a plastic gun bought in a store.

I should hasten to mention that real guns, including B-B guns and air rifles, are *not* toys. They are weapons, plain and simple. As such, they don't belong in the hands of a child, and putting one of them there does nothing but court disaster. If you want to teach a child to aim and shoot, buy him a camera.

Q: If a child asks to participate in an organized sport or take piano lessons and later wants to quit, should parents make the child stick it out?

A: No and maybe.

Children should be free to approach such things as soccer and piano with a spirit of playfulness. In a young child, the initial desire to become involved in a sport or activity is nothing more than expression of curiosity. For this reason, a child should not feel obligated to participate, or continue participating, in a sport or activity because of parental pressure and should, generally speaking, be as free to quit as he is to join. He shouldn't be required to have any better excuse for quitting than "I want to."

Parents who refuse to allow a child to withdraw from something he or she has found unfulfilling unknowingly inhibit the experimental nature of these activities. A child who is not free to quit becomes increasingly reluctant to join for fear of becoming locked into something that might seem attractive at first, but ultimately is not.

A child who's free to leave an activity he entered into of his own initiative is in no danger of developing a "quitter's attitude" toward life. Quite the contrary. The stuff of success—initiative, achievement, motivation, and persistence—grows only when it is allowed to take root and flower within the child. Parents who appropriate these attributes and then attempt to impose them on a child are unintentionally doing more harm than good.

That being the rule, here is the exception: There is occasional value to be had from contracting with a child for specified periods of commitment regarding certain activities, especially those that involve significant monetary investment. For example, parents might require that a child agree to two years of lessons before buying a musical instrument the child has expressed interest in learning to play. In these cases, the child learns something about obligation and responsibility.

To illustrate: Once upon a time, there was a nine-year-old girl named Amy Rosemond who wanted to take piano lessons, so her parents found a teacher, and Amy started taking. Before plunking down for a piano, however, her parents wanted to "wait and see."

After nearly a year, the piano teacher said, "Time to get a piano," and Amy said, "Please, please!" So the daddy called his mother and said, "Grams, you know the family piano that no one plays, well . . ." and Grandma agreed to give the piano to Amy. She even, being the intrepid traveler she is, insisted upon driving the rental truck herself from Chicago to North Carolina. Grandma trusts no one but Grandma.

The daddy and mommy told Amy about her good fortune and said, "Here's the deal. In return for the piano, you must agree to take lessons as long as you live in this house." Amy said that was fine.

So the piano arrived and Amy played merrily away. For about two years, that is. Then the carping started: "I hate piano! I want to quit! I don't like practicing!"

Her mommy and daddy reminded Amy of the agreement, adding, "All it says is you must take lessons. We never said you have to practice. That's between you and your teacher."

So Amy stopped practicing. Her parents said nothing. Six weeks went by when suddenly one sunny day, all over the house the piano was heard playing. Amy's parents said nothing. For six months, Amy played and played. Then the carping started again. Her parents reminded her of the agreement and the playing stopped. But the lessons continued.

Six weeks later, she was heard playing again . . . and that's the way it's been ever since. And all's well with Amy, whether she is playing or not.

Q: Our first child is seven months old. When should we begin reading to her?

A: Last month.

Seriously, folks, a child is never too young for reading. Parents should begin reading to a child by no later than six months of age, but six weeks is even better.

"But," you say, "she might not be able to see the pictures." That's okay. Pictures are not necessary to reading, anyway.

My mother or grandmother read to me every night before bed until I was at least six years old. The books had few pictures. Some had none. I didn't know any better, so I never complained. But I did pay attention, and I did use my imagination. In fact, I probably exercised my imagination lots more than I would have had there been more pictures. I'm not saying that pictures are in any way detrimental, only that they aren't essential.

When I read to Eric and Amy, I generally preferred books with lots of pictures because that forced us to cuddle. The pictures also became the occasion for games of "Show me . . ." and "What's this?"

Early reading stimulates language, perceptual, and cognitive development. Studies have also shown that as a child's communication skills improve, so does motor coordination. This makes sense, not only because an enriching environment stimulates a child's abilities in all areas, but also because language development and motor behavior are interwoven during early childhood.

The nurturing that takes place when a parent reads to a child helps strengthen the child's sense of security. This, in turn, contributes greatly to the growth of independence. Security, independence, and intellectual competence—these form the basis of self-esteem. So you see, early (and ongoing) reading is one of the best investments you can make toward your child's well-being.

Don't, however, confuse the purpose of early reading with teaching a child to read. When you sit down to read to your daughter, do so because it's something you both enjoy. If you start reading to your daughter now and read to her often, you will teach her that reading feels good, and that is quite enough.

It isn't at all unusual for a well-read-to child to suddenly, at age three or four, begin reading. With enough exposure, some children figure out how to read on their own. If they don't and learn to read in first grade, that's okay too.

Begin with books that rhyme, like those by Dr. Seuss. (My favorite rhyming book is Arnold Lobel's *The Man Who Took the Indoors Out.*) The natural rhythm of the words will hold an infant's attention better than prose. Poetry also lends itself to improvisational song, which—assuming you are able to make up and carry a tune—never fails to fascinate and delight the child in us all. Diversify into prose around the same time the child begins talking. Regardless of what you select, follow these guidelines:

—Read to your child at least thirty minutes each day.

—Choose books *you* enjoy reading. The more you like 'em, the more your child will, too!

—Read slightly above your child's current vocabulary level.

—Read with feeling, with gusto! Give each character a different accent! Sing certain passages!

—Hold your child close.

—Have a wonderful time!

For more information and helpful hints on reading aloud to children of all ages, I highly recommend *The Read-Aloud Handbook* by Jim Trelease.

Q: *The preschool program our four-year-old attends has always emphasized social and creative skills, rather than academics. However, the board of directors recently hired a new teacher for the four-year-olds who wants to teach reading and math. According to her, a child this age is ready to begin academic instruction. The parents are divided on this issue, some eager for their children to have a head start, others resisting any changes. What's your opinion?*

A: The fundamental question is "What, if anything, do children gain by learning how to read and perform arithmetic problems at age four?"

The answer: "Nothing."

Take two four-year-olds of approximately equal ability, teach one to read and do basic math, but wait to begin formal instruction with the other until he or she enters first grade. The result? Although the first child might outshine the second through most of first grade, by the time they both reach third grade no one will be able to determine which had the initial advantage.

The concept of readiness is at the crux of the problem. If readiness is defined in terms of whether four-year-olds *can* learn to read and do basic math, then most four-year-olds are ready. If, on the other hand, readiness is defined in terms of the most appropriate time to begin teaching reading and math, then four-year-olds are *not* ready.

The observations and research of Swiss developmental psychologist Jean Piaget (1890–1980) suggest that abstract symbol systems such as those involved in reading and math need not and should not be introduced to children until age six or seven. Piaget maintained that intelligence develops within every human being according to a predictable evolutionary sequence. Each stage of cognitive (intellectual) growth, as characterized by the emergence of new, more sophisticated ways of understanding the world, is built upon previously existing modes of understanding.

John K. Rosemond

Piaget said that any attempt to impose understanding of a certain concept "before its time" was not only fruitless, but potentially harmful. He maintained that if a certain concept was introduced to a child before the appropriate developmental "window" was open, the child might never be able to utilize that concept effectively. Later researchers have argued that teaching four-year-olds to read is accomplished at the expense of doing permanent damage to the very nature of intelligence.

So, if children are not the beneficiaries of the currently popular push for preschool literacy, then why the push? Because it meets the needs of some parents and some teachers, that's why.

Somehow, through a combination of misinformation and misunderstanding, many American parents have decided that since there are few skills more important to success than reading, the earlier a child reads, the better. But early readers serve their parents better than they serve themselves. Early readers calm their parents' anxieties over such things as whether they're smart and whether they'll be good students. Their literacy also stands as a testimonial to the skill and good judgment used in raising them. So the payoff for parents is twofold: They're less worried and their egos are fatter. A powerful payoff, indeed.

Given that parents want their preschoolers to read, a teacher who offers to teach them suddenly becomes a hot item. Everyone scrambles to get their kids into her class. What few seem to realize is that teaching four-year-olds to read is far easier and demands considerably less preparation time, imagination, and energy from a teacher than planning and carrying out a stimulating program of more creative and more developmentally appropriate activities. So the teacher's payoff is also twofold: Less work and a fatter ego.

We seem to be forgetting that education is for the sake of children, not for the sake of adults.

Q: I am an educator who disagrees with your stand on early reading instruction. Recent studies have demonstrated that preschool children have a far greater capacity for learning than was previously suspected. By exposing preschoolers to educational opportunities such as early reading instruction, we acknowledge and nurture this potential.

A: Your argument is the same one that's always been used to justify these programs. Namely: If preschoolers *can* learn to read, then they *should* learn to read. This position is based upon a limited understanding of literacy, as well as limited definitions of learning and achievement.

It's true that reasonably intelligent children as young as three can be taught basic word-recognition skills. But using that to justify teaching preschool children to read is like using the fact that thirteen-year-olds can be taught to drive to justify giving them the opportunity to obtain driver's licenses.

Indeed, preschool children do have a great capacity for learning. And indeed, parents and educators share responsibility for responding appropriately to that potential. The question then becomes, "What kinds of learning experiences are appropriate for preschoolers?"

We know that a preschool child's understanding of the world is earthbound. In other words, it is fairly limited to the universe of concrete, tangible things. Reading involves the intervention of an abstract symbol system—the printed word—to describe tangible and intangible aspects of the universe. Piaget's research tends to indicate that for most children, the critical period for introducing symbol systems of this sort is around age six. In European schools, where this rule-of-thumb is generally practiced, there are few reading problems as compared with the spate that plagues our educational systems. In the Soviet Union, formal education doesn't begin until children are seven, yet Russian children seem none the worse for it.

And just exactly what does it mean to be able to read? Literacy is traditionally defined in terms of an individual's ability to correctly recognize and comprehend words and word passages. If one adheres to this limited definition, then indeed it is possible to induce literacy in preschool children. But any definition of literacy is incomplete unless it also includes the ability to enjoy reading. After all, it matters not that a person can read if he fails to do so for lack of enjoyment. When this third standard is applied to the issue of teaching preschoolers to read, the complete bankruptcy of the idea is revealed.

In *The Hurried Child,* psychologist-author David Elkind cites studies showing that the earlier children are taught to read, the less they enjoy reading and the less they read. Every public school first-grade teacher I've ever discussed this issue with has told me that it is not at all necessary that children come to first grade with more than a basic knowledge of the alphabet. Their only hope is that their young students come to them with a desire to read that's been instilled and reinforced at home.

The trick in helping a child become literate in the complete sense of the term is no trick at all. Here 'tis: Starting as young as six months, read to the child on a regular basis at least thirty minutes a day. There's no better way than this to prepare a child for later reading instruction.

Q: I've put our eight-month-old son in a playpen for short periods during the day ever since he was three months old. Until recently, he's occupied himself quietly until I was able to return. Lately, as soon as I put him in the playpen, he begins screaming bloody murder and doesn't stop until I pick him up. I can't possibly be with him every minute of the day, nor can I let him be free to just roam about the house. The playpen seems like the most sensible and convenient way of solving these problems. On the other hand, he hates the playpen. What can I do?

A: Before we go any further, understand that playpens aren't for play, not in the real sense of the term. Boredom is about all that's possible in a fenced-in area no larger than sixteen-square feet. The more stuff a parent heaps in there to occupy the child, the more cluttered the pen becomes, further restricting the child's ability to interact creatively with his environment (play).

Before they begin crawling, most children will endure the relative isolation of a playpen for brief periods during the day. Crawling, however, stimulates an infant's desire to explore the world. Once a child discovers what excitement there is to be had by moving from one place to another, and then another, getting his hands in the stuff of what's happenin', he's not likely to sit quietly in a playpen. Add to his curiosity the fact that a young toddler (between eight and twelve months) isn't quite sure how much closeness he wants with his mother. This business of getting around on his own is a barrel of monkeys, but it also takes him further away from the one he depends upon the most.

So this-age child is caught in his *own* dilemma. He wants to be with you and he wants to be away from you, doing his own thing. He feels a bit better if he's in control of how much distance there is between you and when separation happens. If *you* walk away, he yells, but if *he* crawls off, it's goodbye. Just to make sure you haven't vaporized while he wasn't looking, he checks on you every few minutes. When you put him in a playpen, his anxiety level goes up. Not only isn't he controlling the separation, but he can't get to you when he needs to.

I'd like to digress a moment and say a few things about ducks. Several days after they hatch, a brood of ducklings will line up behind their mother and follow her wherever she goes. This is called *imprinting*. After a few weeks of parading about in this fashion, they break away and begin fending more or less for themselves.

European biologist Niko Tinbergen wanted to see what would happen if the imprinting process was tampered with. He placed small barriers around a circular track where mother ducks walked. As their babies followed, they had to scramble over the barriers to keep up. The result: These frustrated ducklings persisted in following their mothers long after other, non-frustrated ducklings had moved off on their own.

Before a child can begin making motions of independence, he must know, beyond the shadow of a doubt, that his mother will be easily accessible in time of need. Playpens frustrate the newly mobile child the same way Tinbergen's barriers frustrated the ducklings. And as was the case with the ducklings, frustration makes a child more determined to keep his mother close.

So, by using a playpen to contain (for whatever reason) a child who has started moving about under his own steam, you increase the likelihood that he will cling to you long after most children have become more self-sufficient.

One of the nicest gifts you can give your child, once he begins crawling, is a childproofed living area where he can crawl and putter and get into safe, unbreakable things to his heart's content while you relax, knowing he's all right. He'll experience the same insecurities as other post-crawlers, but instead of getting stuck, he'll go right through them.

Q: Our sixteen-month-old daughter has recently started climbing and getting into lots of things that are "off limits." We have tried popping her hand whenever she picks up something we don't want her to handle, but that doesn't seem to faze her and often makes her even more determined! How would you suggest we go about keeping her out of mischief?

A: The most effective way of keeping your daughter out of mischief is to remove the potential for mischief by childproofing. Childproofing a home protects the child from danger and valuables from breakage while at the same time providing the child with an open, stimulating environment in which to explore to his/her heart's content.

Take inventory, room by room, of things dangerous or valuable that are within your daughter's reach. Put childproof latches on lower cabinets, childproof covers on electrical outlets, and place gates across staircases. Bring down to your daughter's level things she can touch. Give her a cabinet of her own in the kitchen and stock it with things like wooden spoons, pots, empty thread spools, boxes, flexible straws, and anything else that might fascinate her and help stimulate creative behavior. If you do a good job, you should be able to let your daughter roam around the house with much less supervision than you've previously provided.

When she's about thirty months of age, you can begin slowly restoring your home to its previous state. Introduce one valuable at a time, first letting your daughter see and feel the item, then putting it where it belongs and letting her know it's not a plaything. The discrimination between "can touch" and "can't touch" is easily made at this age, as long as parents don't introduce too many interesting things at any one time.

Here's a tip for parents of toddlers when the youngster picks up something fragile, like a piece of valuable crystal: The child is almost certain to drop and break the item if an adult puts on a horrified expression, says "Give me that!" and moves rapidly toward the child with arms outstretched, hands open like claws. Panic breeds panic. Instead, control your fears, stay in one spot, squat down so you're at eye-level with the child, put a smile on your face, extend your hand palm-up and say, "Ooooh, how pretty! Will you put it in my hand so I can see, too?"

If you've done a good acting job, the child will smile in return and place the item gently in your palm. Let the child know this wasn't a trick by putting her on your lap and examining the object together for a minute or so before getting up and saying, "I'm going to put this up here so we can both look at it. Isn't it pretty?" This procedure satisfies the child's curiosity, saves money, and helps build a cooperative, rather than antagonistic, parent-child relationship.

Q: Our three-year-old daughter has recently invented, and is spending lots of time with, an imaginary playmate she calls "Cindy." Her obsession with Cindy is beginning to go a bit far, I think. She wants me to set a place for her at the dinner table and invite her along whenever we leave the house. When I've suggested that Cindy doesn't really exist, my daughter has become extremely angry and upset. Do I have reason to be concerned, or is this just a passing phase?

A: Your daughter's fascination with her imaginary friend is just a passing phase, but an important one. Rather than being worried, you should be glad.

Fantasy thinking emerges around age three. Like any other mental attribute, imagination must be exercised in order to strengthen and grow. Cindy is your daughter's way of doing just that. She's taking a very important step toward the eventual mastery of abstract thinking. Also, since an active imagination is essential to reading comprehension, Cindy is actually helping your daughter toward eventually becoming a successful reader.

Trying to debate the issue of Cindy's existence with your daughter is a lost cause. To a three-year-old, if something can be imagined, then that something truly exists. In your daughter's eyes and mind, Cindy is as real as you are. Three-year-olds invest a considerable amount of security in their imaginary playmates. They *need* them. No wonder your daughter became upset when you tried to reason away Cindy's existence. Just as your adult mind cannot comprehend your daughter's obsession with Cindy, her child's mind can't understand your failure to accept Cindy's existence. So call it a draw and stop worrying.

At this stage of her life, your daughter is starting to form relationships with other children. Cindy enables her to practice social skills in a safe, nonthreatening context, thus strengthening your daughter's ability to interact successfully with other children. When your daughter and another child play together with Cindy, they're practicing small-group social skills.

The more your daughter plays with Cindy, the fewer demands she makes of your time and energy. Instead of relying on you for occupation, she's relying on Cindy, which effectively means she is relying on herself. The more self-reliant and resourceful your daughter becomes, the better sense of self-esteem she will have.

Any way you look at it, Cindy is probably one of the best things that's ever happened to your daughter. Her invisible friend is contributing to almost every aspect of her growth and development. Instead of worrying about Cindy, relax and count your blessings.

POINT
SIX

Television and Children: More than Meets the Eye

Between birthdays two and six, the average American preschool child watches thirty hours of television a week. This isn't a number I pulled out of thin air, but one that's been confirmed by Nielsen survey after Nielsen survey since the early 1970s.

Thirty hours a week is slightly more than four hours a day, which could take place thusly: One-half hour of cartoons before leaving for preschool, one hour of "Sesame Street" in the morning, another half-hour of cartoons in the afternoon, followed by "Mister Rogers" and a "Leave It to Beaver" rerun, the "Muppets," and a family sitcom in the evening. Not at all out of the ordinary.

By multiplying thirty hours of television a week times fifty-two weeks, you discover that the average American preschooler watches 1,560 hours of television a year, for a grand total of 6,240 hours between the ages of two and six. Based on a fourteen-hour day, this means that preschool children spend roughly one-third of their daily discretionary time sitting in front of a television set.

Now, you may already be saying, "That's not my child! My

child watches no more than fifteen hours of television a week." That's a perfectly understandable reaction, but I'm going to burst your bubble. Studies have also shown that most parents tend to underestimate their children's television viewing time by approximately 50 percent. So, if you think your child is watching fifteen hours of television a week, the actual number is probably much higher than that—perhaps even as high as that average of thirty. On the other hand, if you insist, let's say your preschool child watches an average of "only" fifteen hours a week. That means he or she will have watched 3,120 hours by age six. Does that make you feel more comfortable?

In order to fully appreciate what these numbers mean, you must understand that your child's preschool years and, in particular, those four years from age two to age six, are among the most important years of his/her life. Developmental psychologists and educators refer to them as the "formative years." They are called "formative" because they comprise that period during which the young child is discovering, developing, and strengthening the skills he/she will need to become a creative, competent person.

How Not *to Raise a Gifted Child*

Nearly every human being is born already programmed for giftedness of nearly every conceivable form—intellectual, artistic, musical, athletic, interpersonal, spiritual, and so on. During the formative years, these programs are activated by exposing the young child to environments and experiences which "push the right genetic buttons," so to speak.

In other words, releasing the richness of each child's developmental birthright simply requires that the child have sufficient opportunities for exploration, discovery, and imaginative play. Environments and experiences which stimulate and exercise the young child's emerging skills are, therefore, compatible with his/her developmental needs. On the other hand, environments which fail to offer these important opportunities are incompatible. And time is of the essence. Developmental research has consistently demonstrated that a child has approximately six years in which to "get in touch" with the many basic skills that comprise competency and creativity. The formative years are the "window of opportunity" for giftedness. A child of six who, for lack of opportunity, is deficient with respect to one or more aspects of giftedness will probably always have problems in those areas.

When a child sits and becomes absorbed in watching television, that television becomes his/her audiovisual environment. Since the average American child spends more time watching television than doing any other single thing during his formative years, we must conclude that television has become a primary environment for our children and will, therefore, influence their development in significant, far-reaching ways.

The question, then, becomes: "Does television create/constitute a healthy or unhealthy environment for children?"

For the past thirty years or more, social scientists have been attempting to answer that very question. Their research has focused almost exclusively on the effects of television's content—whether, for instance, a program is violent or nonviolent, sexy or not—on the social behavior of children. This has had unfortunate consequences, because the average American parent has been led to believe that television's only danger to children is a matter of theme. If a child is watching "Sesame Street" or a family sitcom, we tend to think there's no harm. On the other hand, if the child is watching a program that contains themes of sex and/or violence, we're probably going to turn the television off, change the channel, or send the child from the room. Because of this tendency to judge the "book" of television by its cover, American parents are largely unaware of the more insidious and far more damaging influence of television-watching as a *process*, independent of the content of the programs being watched.

In order to see firsthand what I'm talking about, the next time your child is watching television, look at *him* instead of the program. As they say, a picture is worth more than a thousand words. Check out the illustration on the next page.

Not a pretty sight, is it? Now, ask yourself, "What is he doing?" The answer, of course, is, "Nothing." Not one competency skill, not one gift, is being exercised.

Regardless of the program, therefore, television-watching inhibits the development of initiative, curiosity, resourcefulness, creativity, motivation, imagination, reasoning and problem-solving abilities, communication skills, social skills, fine and gross-motor skills, and eye-hand coordination. Shall I go on? Because television causes the child to stare at, rather than scan, the environment, it's safe to add that visual tracking skills are not being strengthened.

Furthermore, television-watching interferes significantly with the development of a long attention span. Many people mistakenly believe that if a child can sit mesmerized in front of a television set for two or three hours at a stretch, he must have— or at least be developing—a long attention span. That's an "optical illusion." Consider the fact that the picture on a television screen changes, on the average, about every three to four seconds. Because of this constant perceptual shift, or "flicker," the television-watching child isn't attending to any one thing for longer than a few seconds. As a result, television-watching is a strangely paradoxical situation for the young child. The more time he spends watching television, the shorter his attention span becomes.

Last, but by no means least, because the action on a television set shifts constantly and capriciously backward, forward, and laterally in time (not to mention from subject matter to subject matter), television fails to promote logical, sequential thinking, which is essential to an understanding of cause-and-effect relationships. This causes difficulties in both following directions and anticipating consequences.

Once again, these failings are the same regardless of whether the child is watching "Sesame Street," an adult movie on late-night cable, or a video rental. In each case, the child is watching in the same passive manner. This means that for the preschool child, program content is a largely irrelevant issue as far as that child's development is concerned.

As I said earlier, the preschool child's competency skills emerge and begin developing through exercise. During the formative years, play is the natural form this exercise takes. But a child watching television isn't playing. In fact, he isn't doing anything competent at all. Every hour, therefore, that a preschool child spends watching television is an hour of that child's potential being wasted.

Examined from a developmental perspective, one is forced to conclude that television-watching is a deprivational experience for the young child. It deprives him of the opportunity to discover and take delight in developing his natural potential for giftedness. And the sad fact is, that once that "window of opportunity" closes, it can never again be fully opened.

But don't just take my word for it. As with everything else, the proof has got to be in the pudding. I'm saying that if a child spends a significant amount of time during his formative years parked in front of a television set, he's likely to be much less competent than he would otherwise have been. If watching television diminishes a child's potential for competency, then there ought to be evidence that television-generation children are less competent than children of previous generations. Does such evidence exist? Indeed, it does.

John K. Rosemond

Television Disabilities

Since 1955, when American children began watching significant amounts of television, scholastic achievement test scores have steadily declined. As a nation, our literacy level has declined as well. Today, nearly one of every five seventeen-year-olds in this country is functionally illiterate, meaning he/she cannot read with comprehension at a fifth-grade level. The functionally illiterate individual cannot read a newspaper, a recipe, or a manual for operating a power tool. Both of these trends become even more alarming when one considers that academic standards are lower today than they were in 1955. Today's fifth-grade reader, for instance, is comparable to a third-grade reader from 1955.

To top it off, since 1955, learning disabilities have become nearly epidemic in our schools, both public and private. Learning disabled children are children who can't seem to get it all together when it comes to learning the basic academic skills of reading and writing. Some researchers estimate that as many as three out of ten children in our schools today are learning disabled to one degree or another. Interestingly enough, the symptoms that characterize a population of learning-disabled children and the list of developmental deficiencies inherent to the television-watching experience are one and the same.

Learning-disabled children often have visual-scanning problems. Their eyes fail to smoothly scan a line of print from left to right. They tend to exhibit problems with eye-hand coordination as well as fine- and gross-motor skills. They are often not proficient at tasks requiring active problem-solving (reading, for example). They are frequently deficient with respect to active-listening and communication skills. They often display social adjustment difficulties. Their teachers typically report that they have difficulty following a sequence of directions or the steps involved in solving a problem. They are frequently described by their teachers as passive and easily frustrated by challenges. They tend to be unimaginative (and imagination is essential to reading comprehension). Last, but not least, almost all learning-disabled children have short attention spans.

In short, an almost perfect parallel exists between the list of competency skills that television fails to exercise and the symptoms characteristic of a population of learning-disabled children. But learning disabilities are just the tip of the iceberg. Again and again, veteran teachers—those who are in the best position to have seen the steady decline in competency skills I've been talking about—tell me that today's children are, as a rule, less resourceful, less imaginative, and not nearly as motivated as the children they knew and taught in pre-television time. They also tell me that the average child's attention span seems to have significantly shortened since the early 1950s.

I know a woman who taught second grade in public schools for forty-four years—from 1934 until 1978. In her early years, she would bring her students back from lunch and read them stories from books that had few, if any, pictures. Up through the 1940s and early 1950s, her story time lasted one hour. In the late 1950s, however, she began noticing that most of her children were no longer able to sit still and pay attention for that length of time. So, around 1960, she cut her story "hour" to thirty minutes. By the mid-1960s, even though she was now reading from books that had pictures on every page, she again cut story time to fifteen minutes. In 1972, because her students were unable to sit and pay attention for longer than three to five minutes, she eliminated story time altogether.

I've heard stories similar to this from nearly every veteran teacher with whom I've ever talked. And I'm not at all surprised. You take a child whose formative years have been dominated by television—a child whose competency skills are weak because television has pacified nearly every aspect of his inborn potential for competency—and you put that child in a classroom where the learning expected of him demands resourcefulness, initiative, curiosity, motivation, imagination, eye-hand coordination, active listening, adequate communication skills, functional reasoning and problem-solving skills, and a long attention span, and the distinct possibility exists that that child is going to have problems of learning and performance in school.

It would be a gross oversimplification to imply that television alone is responsible for the plague of learning and motivation problems in our schools. Likewise, it would be naive of any of us to ignore the obvious connection between the deficiencies inherent to the *process* of television-watching and the deficiencies in competency skills that characterize not only the learning-disabled child, but seemingly this entire generation of television-overdosed children. Keep in mind also that no other single influence has so dramatically altered the nature of childhood in the last forty years than the television set.

Questions?

Q: What guidelines do you recommend parents use when deciding how much television to let children watch?

A: First of all, I don't believe there's any justification for letting a preschool child watch any television at all. In fact, I think it makes utmost sense to keep a child completely away from television until he or she has learned to read, reads fairly well, and enjoys reading. For most children, that point will be reached between the third and fifth grades. Once literacy has been fairly well-established, I see no problem with letting a child watch programs which represent the world in a realistic manner and which broaden the child's understanding of the world, his or her relationship to it, and how it works. Nature specials, documentaries, historically-based movies, sports, and cultural events all fit this criteria. Programs such as these open up the child's view of the world and stimulate him to want to go to the library and find out more about what he's seen, be it whales, baseball, or the Civil War. Regardless of the quality of the programs being watched, however, I strongly recommend that parents not allow children to watch any more than five hours of television a week.

Q: What about programs like "Sesame Street" and "Mister Rogers"?

A: All television programs, regardless of their content, are watched in the same passive manner. From this perspective, "Sesame Street" is as much a one-way street as any other program by any other name.

Programs like "Sesame Street" appeal to parents because of their supposed educational value for children. But the notion that preschool children can learn the alphabet, numerals, and even a basic reading vocabulary from "Sesame Street" is nothing more than hype, brought to you by the same folks who tell us that a certain toothpaste will make us more appealing to persons of the opposite sex. My reaction to the salespitch for "Sesame Street" is simply, "So what?"

First, there's no trick to teaching children these pre-academic skills. Second, children don't need to know them before they go to school. Third, a classroom provides a much more appropriate and effective environment for learning basic skills (see Point Five for further discussion).

Studies have consistently failed to demonstrate that "Sesame Street" imparts any lasting academic advantage to its young consumers. In fact, a 1975 study conducted by the Russell Sage Foundation concluded that heavy viewers of "Sesame Street" demonstrated fewer gains in cognitive skills than light viewers.

When this issue comes up during one of my workshops or in the question-and-answer period at the end of a presentation, I ask the folks in the audience to raise their hands if they learned to read soon after starting school. Everyone raises their hands. I then ask for a show of hands from those folks who watched "Sesame Street" during their preschool years. No hands go up, but everyone starts to laugh. In other words, "Sesame Street" is not a necessary prerequisite to learning to read.

"Mister Rogers" is a horse of a slightly different color. Although I feel that Fred Rogers's program makes no essential contribution to a child's overall development, it has its merits. In the first place, instead of pushing "academics," Rogers strives to heighten a child's awareness of the environment and encourage curiosity and exploration. His aims, therefore, are consistent with the developmental needs of his viewing audience. In the second place, Rogers establishes as personal a relationship with the children in his viewing audience as the medium allows. I sense that every child feels that Rogers is talking directly with him or her. Finally, to my knowledge, "Mister Rogers" is the only show on television that uses primarily one camera. Consequently, the hyperactive "flicker" that is characteristic of other television programs is absent. Besides having a calmer influence on a child than programs like "Sesame Street," this also means "Mister Rogers" encourages a much longer attention span.

Q: Television may not be doing anything wonderful for my two small children, but it certainly helps me get some time to myself during the day. Besides, I still fail to see how a few hours a day spent watching programs like "Sesame Street" or "Electric Company" can harm a child's mind. Have you ever tried to keep small children entertained all day, every day?

A: You are sadly mistaken if you think television is doing you or your children any favors. The more a young child watches television, the more that child will eventually come to depend upon it as a primary source of occupation and entertainment. Every dependency encumbers the growth of self-reliance. The young child who becomes dependent upon television will, when the television is off, seek to satisfy that dependency in other ways. Predictably, he transfers it to the next most available and receptive object/person, and Mom is usually right up there at the top of the list.

A vicious cycle quickly develops. The more the child watches television, the more television pacifies his or her initiative, resourcefulness, imagination, and creativity. When the television is off, instead of finding something with which to entertain himself, he looks for Mom to take over where the television left off. He complains of being bored, he whines for Mom to find something for him to do, he demands that she become his playmate. Partly out of fear that the child will interpret any denial as rejection, Mom is at first likely to cooperate with these complaints and demands. But when it becomes obvious that the child can't get enough of her, Mom begins looking for an excuse to let him watch television. Any excuse will do, but "Sesame Street" is one of the "best."

There you have it. The child becomes increasingly addicted

to watching television and his mother becomes increasingly addicted to letting him watch. Little does she realize that this strategy is slowly eroding the only thing that will ever give her and her child the independence they need from one another, and that is her child's ability to do for himself.

What, pray tell, did children do before television? Why, they found things to do, that's what! Weather permitting, they went outside to play. They made mud pies and built forts out of tree branches and skipped stones across ponds and played "It" and "Mother May I?" and pretended to be all sorts of heroes and heroines and damsels in distress and they rarely, if ever, complained of having nothing to do. Remember? It is the television-generation child who complains of having nothing to do. When are we going to wake up and realize that this isn't a coincidence?

Q: Our five-month old loves to look at television. While I watch my programs in the evening, she lies on her quilt and stares at the screen. I think she likes the play of movement, brightness, and color on the screen, but I'm beginning to worry that her fascination with the television could become a habit. I know it is detrimental for children to watch too much television, that it can hurt their powers of imagination and creativity, not to mention their reading ability. Can her early interest in the television become habit? Should I cut back my own watching on her behalf? When, if ever, is it all right to let her start watching?

A: In answer to your first question: Television is definitely habit-forming. The earlier a habit is formed, the more it influences the individual's attitudes and behavior. I would think, therefore, by letting your infant daughter stare at the television screen for significant periods of time, that you are increasing the possibility that she will someday become a television junkie.

Movement, brightness, and color may play a part in your daughter's fascination with watching television, but the key element in her growing attachment—and possible eventual addiction—is the constant shifting of perspective and picture. If you pay attention, you will notice that the picture on the screen changes, or "flickers" every few seconds.

The flicker is there to maintain the interest of the viewer. It "hooks" the viewer's attention and holds him in its seductively hypnotic embrace. The constant flickering of the screen is stimulating in a pleasant sort of way, and positive stimulation amounts to reward. In effect, each flicker is the equivalent of an electronic M&M, positively reinforcing the viewer for his increasing passivity. When we say that a person is "glued to the tube," we aren't far from fact.

In the language of psychology, television puts the viewer on a "variable interval schedule" of reinforcement. Variable because the interval between flickers isn't constant, reinforcing because each flicker is pleasantly stimulating. Now, listen to this passage from a contemporary psychology text: "Research indicates that learning under variable reward conditions lasts longer than learning under any other reward schedule." In other words, variable rewards result in the formation of persistent and possibly lifelong habits.

So, is your daughter in danger of becoming a television addict? Most definitely. Should you curtail your own watching on her behalf? I'd recommend it, but how about on your own behalf as well? You might use the time to read. Not only would reading enrich your own life, but studies also show that young children who often see their parents reading become better readers than children whose parents rarely read.

When is it all right to let a child start watching television? I personally don't believe that a child should watch any television at all until he or she can read well. After that time, there's no real harm in letting a child watch up to five hours of television a week, preferably programs that expand his or her understanding of the real world.

Q: My husband and I are seeing a psychologist because of discipline problems with our six-year-old son. Charlie has also had problems in school this year, namely concentrating and finishing work. The psychologist recently told us that part of Charlie's problem is attention-deficit disorder, which he said is the new term for hyperactivity. He said Charlie's short attention span is causing most of the problems at school and is contributing to many of the problems we are having with him at home. We agree that Charlie is impulsive and very difficult to control, but are somewhat confused about the atten-tion span thing. If, as the psychologist said, Charlie can't control his attention-span problem, then why is he able to sit quietly and watch television for two or three hours at a stretch. In fact, television is just about the only thing that will keep him quiet. The psychologist had no explanation for that. Do you?

A: The fact that Charlie can watch television for two to three hours doesn't contradict a diagnosis of attention-deficit disor-der. Television holds Charlie's interest in a way the everyday world doesn't because the picture on a television screen changes every few seconds.

Not only is television's flicker highly stimulating, it also has a mesmerizing, or hypnotic, effect upon the viewer. This is television's "hook," created through the use of anywhere from three to five cameras in the production studio. Some people seem better able to resist the bait than others, but children are especially susceptible. Furthermore, television's constantly shifting perspective is perfectly suited to a child with attention-deficit disorder.

Although you find that television keeps Charlie quiet, it's actually making his attention-span problems worse, rather than better. He can watch television for three hours and not have to watch any one thing for longer than about ten seconds, four seconds being the norm. In other words, television is actually reinforcing Charlie's short attention span. The longer he watches, the more his short attention span becomes habit.

Where else in the real world does the scene in front of you flicker every few seconds? Nowhere. So the perceptual habits Charlie develops while watching television will be worthless, even harmful, in other environments, particularly school.

In my experience, the most effective treatment plan for children with moderate to severe cases of attention-deficit dis-order involves a combination of behavioral interventions along with a medication such as Ritalin to assist in impulse control and the development of a longer attention span. In addition, I always recommend that these kids be allowed to watch no more than three hours of television a week. Preferably, this should consist primarily of shows like nature documentaries, where the content, rather than the production technique, is the "hook."

Q: Our eight-year-old son has a learning disability that handicaps his ability to pay attention, follow directions, and correctly decipher the printed word. He's already more than a year behind in reading skills. We recently watched a talk show featuring a specialist in learning disabilities who said most, if not all, learning disabilities are inherited. Is there a way of finding out for sure whether Billy's disability is inherited?

A: The fact is, learning disabilities come in many varieties and no one knows for certain what causes any given one. Some may be inherited, or at least related in some way to genetic factors. Even if there was a way of making this determination, I don't think "bad genes" would be found to account for more than a small minority.

Since the early 1950s, learning disabilities have become epidemic among school-age children in America. Many say the sharp increase is due to better identification procedures. That argument doesn't make a lot of sense. Better identification procedures don't cause epidemics; they come about as a result of them. I think we've had to put more effort into research and identification *because* of the increase.

It's interesting to note that learning disabilities are not nearly as much a problem in European school-age populations as they are in the United States. Since we share much of the same gene pool, this would seem to minimize a genetic explanation and suggest that the reason for this country's epidemic may be largely environmental.

The question then becomes: "What are the most typical differences in upbringing between European and American children?"

There are many, but one of the most striking has to do with television. By and large, European children watch less than five hours of television a week, and American children watch between twenty-five and thirty. Can large amounts of television cause learning disabilities? Developmental theory strongly suggests it can.

A vast array of skills and talents is contained within the human genetic code. In order to activate this program, the preschool child must be exposed to environments and experiences that promote the exercise of those talents. In other words, the more creatively active the child is during his or her preschool—or formative—years, the more talented he or she will eventually be.

Watching television is a passivity, not an activity. It does not *properly* engage human potential—whether it be motor, intellectual, creative, social, sensory, verbal, or emotional. Therefore, by its very nature, and regardless of the program, television is a deprivational experience for the preschool child.

Reading is not one skill, but a collection of skills. In order to learn to read well, a child must come to the task with the complete collection. If pieces of the puzzle are missing or damaged, learning to read will be that much more frustrating for the child.

Remember that the average American child has watched 6,000-plus hours of television before he enters first grade. Think of it! Can we truly expect that the puzzle can endure that amount of developmental deprivation and survive intact? And let us not forget that learning-disabled children are only the tip of the "Why-Can't-Johnny-Read?" iceberg. Since the early 1950s, scholastic achievement measures have slipped steadily downhill and illiteracy among seventeen-year-olds has risen to 20 percent.

Could our love affair with television be lurking behind our national reading crisis? We may never know for sure. The question is, is it worth the risk?

Q: Is there any truth to the idea that watching violence on television can make children more violent?

A: In the mid-sixties, a growing number of people became concerned about television's preoccupation with murder and mayhem. In particular, the question was asked, "What possible adverse effects could a daily dose of video violence have on the impressionable minds of America's children?"

The Report to the Surgeon General on Television and Social

Behavior, published in 1972, verified that children can, and often do, act on the suggestion, inherent in the themes of many television programs, that violence is an acceptable way of handling conflict and other problem situations. The idea that violence on television can stimulate violence on the playground has since become a generally accepted belief.

But the tie that could forever bind television violence to aggressive behavior in children has yet to be found. The so-called "smoking gun" theory is still just a theory.

No matter. After all, the public has a scapegoat on which to hang the growing threat of juvenile aggression; consumer advocacy groups, like Action for Children's Television, have a drum to beat; and the networks can demonstrate their sensitivity to social issues by reducing violence on television. In the final analysis, all this brouhaha costs the networks nothing.

There's definitely reason to suspect a link between television and aggressive behavior among children. Since the early 1950s, when television first moved into our homes, the number of violent crimes attributed to juveniles has increased more than tenfold. Over the same period, big-city public schools have become a battleground, where students fight not only among themselves, but also with their teachers. Even without a final answer from the scientific establishment, the anecdotal evidence strongly suggests that the "television generation" is also a more violent generation.

Efforts to prove (or disprove) the "smoking gun" theory, however, might be exercises in barking up the wrong tree. The relationship between television and aggressive behavior in children may have more to do with process than content—more to do with the watching than with what's being watched.

Animal behaviorist Harry Harlow of the University of Wisconsin isolated juvenile chimpanzees in environments that offered no opportunities for play. He observed unusually violent behavior in these chimps when he reunited them with normally reared peers.

Psychologist Jerome Singer of Yale University has found evidence that children who engage in frequent fantasy play are less likely to be aggressive and hostile and better able to tolerate frustration than children who, for whatever reasons, do not engage in make-believe games.

Joseph Chilton Pearce, author of *Magical Child*, writes that play is the most important of all childhood activities. It is through active, imaginative play, Pearce says, that a child develops "creative competence," or mastery of his environment.

In his latest book, *The Bond of Power*, Pearce adds that children who are not allowed extensive playtime or whose play is restricted to forms prescribed by adults (e.g., store-bought toys, adult-supervised activities), develop feelings of isolation and come to perceive the world as a threat instead of a challenge. Anxiety causes them to either withdraw or attempt to control the world by force. In this regard, it's interesting to note that the incidence of depression, long regarded by psychiatrists and psychologists as violence turned within, is also on the rise among our nation's children.

The average American child, while he sits and stares at thirty hours of television a week, is not playing in *any* sense of the term. He is not doing anything but watching, which is hardly doing anything at all. If play, especially fantasy play, is as essential to the formation of a healthy personality as Harlow, Singer, and Pearce think, then television is fundamentally unhealthy for children, regardless of the program being watched.

It is distinctly, and disturbingly, possible that television can so isolate a child from the world (while seeming to bring the world closer), that rage or retreat are, ultimately, his only options.

Q: Our board of education has just approved the installation of computers in the schools. Several questions remain, one of which is whether to make computer-assisted education available to children at all levels of instruction. As you might expect, there is no consensus on this issue. The "progressives" are in favor of computers at every grade level; the "purists" argue for a traditional education during the elementary years (K-6). We would like to know where you stand on this issue.

A: I stand slightly left of purist and considerably right of progressive. Computer-assisted education at the early elementary level (K-3) isn't sensible, necessary, or practical.

Like any other set of abilities, intellectual skills unfold according to an immutable maturation sequence. Each stage of growth develops upon previous ones and forms the framework for successive ones. Furthermore, each stage is compatible with and nurtured by certain forms of learning. Harm can be done by either failure to provide appropriate forms or by imposing inappropriate ones.

Computers present an inappropriate instructional format for early elementary children because, for the most part, a pre-fourth grade child's cognitive abilities are not mature enough for either (1) the level of learning technology represented by a computer, or (2) the level of abstraction inherent to the computer-learning process.

It may not make developmental sense to put computers in early elementary classrooms, but I'm not at all surprised at the general eagerness to do so. It is typically American to try to pull the maturational horse behind a cart full of technological hardware.

I notice that several computer companies are pushing software for children as young as two or three, along with the insinuation that if your child isn't "computer-literate" by the time he enters school, he'll forever be a cultural cripple. This is the latest farce from Madison Avenue, the same bunch who bring you soaps that keep your hands looking younger, longer, and more equally delirious nonsense. Need I tell you that people who write advertising copy aren't interested in your child?

At a recent seminar sponsored by several big corporations, the question was raised, "How important is it that elementary children become familiar with computers?" The consensus: Not important. The technology is changing so rapidly that whatever children learn now will have to be unlearned when they enter the marketplace. The fact is, our public schools simply don't have the resources to keep up with the innovations. Furthermore, programming and design are the only two really marketable computer skills. Depending on the software package involved, virtually anyone can be taught to operate a computer in anywhere from three hours to three days. Definitely, computers are here to stay and schools have a responsibility to familiarize children with them, but not to act as if their lives and/or livelihood depend upon it.

Since, in the history of our species, written and print communication evolved before computers, it seems logical to require that a youngster attain a certain level of proficiency in reading, writing, and arithmetic before graduating to computer-learning. For instance, if we set fourth-grade achievement as the standard, some children would be ready in second grade, others not until much later.

In his landmark book, *The Disappearance of Childhood*, Neil Postman makes the point that mastery of traditional literacy skills (reading and writing) are essential to maintaining an important—nay, *vital*—distinction between adulthood and childhood. Television and other electric media, Postman says, erase this distinction and render it meaningless.

I have no doubt that computers represent a quantum leap in human tool-making and that their benefits are limited only by our vision. But unless that vision incorporates and is tempered by an appreciation for what childhood is all about, we risk doing more harm than good to our children—and, therefore, ourselves—with this new technology. With this in mind, a few words from nineteenth-century education philosopher Thomas Dewey seem appropos: "If we identify ourselves with the real instincts and needs of childhood, and (require) only (their) fullest assertion and growth . . . discipline and culture of adult life shall all come in their due season."

Q: *We recently bought a popular and expensive video game unit for our eight-year-old son. Actually, he earned it by making good grades in school. We're beginning to think we made a mistake, however, because all he wants to do is play it. We've also seen some disturbing personality changes—a lower tolerance for frustration, temper tantrums, more conflict with his younger brother, talking back to us— and wonder if they could be related to his obsession with the video games. Unfortunately, we don't see how we can take it away, or even put limits on it without seeming to break our promise. Any suggestions?*

A: You're not alone. I've heard the same story of regret from lots of parents.

I said it in 1982, when the first wave of the video game craze hit, and I'll say it again: At the very least, these devices are worthless. At most, they are dangerous. The younger the child, the greater the potential for danger. (Before I go any further, I need to distinguish between the type of video games that are included in educational software and video games that are noneducational. My remarks pertain exclusively to the latter.)

In the first place, video games are *not* toys. By definition, a toy is something that provides opportunity for creative, imaginative play as well as constructive learning. Not only are video games noncreative and nonconstructive, they're also stressful.

I've watched lots of children, including my own, "play" video games. They don't look like they're having fun. Typically, the body is tense, the facial expression strained. Then there's the howl of protest, if not temper tantrum, when the *"Game Over!"* sign flashes. If this is fun, things have certainly changed since I was a kid. I'd call this "Type A" behavior.

In the second place, video games lead to addictive behavior. In this case, the "high" is a high score. The problem is, no score is ever high enough. As in a drug addiction, where the addict must constantly increase his dose in order to feel satisfied, the video-game addicted child becomes obsessed with constantly increasing his score.

A situation of this sort can lead to exactly the kinds of behavior and personality changes you describe. Put a child, or any human being for that matter, in a stress-producing environment for long periods of time, and you're going to see negative behavior changes. Prolonged stress lowers an individual's tolerance for frustration and increases the likelihood of conflict in relationships as well as other acting-out behaviors. Eventually, the individual's coping skills break down completely. Keep in mind also that children are far more vulnerable than adults to the effects of stress.

In conclusion, I don't think you should have bought your son a video game unit in the first place. But, you've raised a good point: Since you promised you would, what can you do now?

You can limit his game-time to, for instance, thirty minutes a day on nonschool days only. Or, better yet, you can tell him, "We made a mistake," and take it away completely. Perhaps he'd agree to let you sell it and replace it with something of equal dollar-value (but greater play-value), like a new bike. The additional expense would be worth it, believe me.

Q: For two years, with little success, I have tried to limit my children's television time. I have three problems which are stopping me. First, there's a husband who loves to watch television and won't cooperate in any plan that interferes with his "freedom of watching," as he so eloquently puts it. Second, even without the first problem, I haven't come up with a way of enforcing the limits I set. Third, there's the even more fundamental problem of answering the question, "How much is too much?" for children who are four and eight. So, what about it?

A: In 1978, I suggested to Willie that we curtail the time Eric and Amy were spending in front of the television. In fact, I argued for cutting their television time back from the nearly twenty-five hours a week they were watching to zero—cold turkey!

Like your husband, Willie enjoyed watching television and, though she agreed to eliminating television for the children, she didn't want to give up her favorite shows. After much discussion, we came up with what we felt was the ideal solution: We moved the television into our bedroom. There, Willie could watch whenever and whatever she wanted without having to be on the alert for children trying to sneak looks. Several months later, the television broke, and we let it stay that way for nearly four years. During that time, we all learned that without a television, the quality of life in our family was better in every respect.

Q: What changes did you see in your children during the four years that you didn't have a television?

A: When we removed the television, Eric was making mediocre grades in school, he didn't like to read, had no particular interests, and often complained of being bored. Amy's grades were better than her brother's, but she only read what she had to for school and had become a world-class "couch potato."

After reading Marie Winn's excellent and eye-opening book, *ThePlug-In Drug* (highly recommended!), Willie and I moved the television out of their lives, and eventually ours as well. After about three months of hearing what mean parents we were, we began to notice a definite change for the better in both children's behavior and attitude. To begin with, they stopped complaining of having nothing to do. They became more outgoing, communicative, and affectionate. They became more active socially, and we saw marked improvement in their social skills. They stopped bickering at each other as often. We saw a definite improvement in their senses of humor. They began reading more and even asking to go to the library. When we'd go to the shopping mall, they'd ask to go to the bookstore instead of the toystore. Their grades improved, Eric's in particular.

But by far the very best result of removing television from their lives was that both children began acting like children again. Their play became more creative and imaginative. Amy would, for instance, spend entire afternoons acting out the parts to various story records. Eric built forts and log cabins in the woods behind our house.

Within a year, both kids had developed hobbies which they are very much involved with to this day. Eric became quite skilled at building models, and particularly interested in World War II military equipment. He would purchase a model, then go to the library and research how and where it was used, how it was painted, and so on. When he'd done his homework, he'd build the model, airbrush it to achieve an authentic look, then build a diorama within which to display it. Each model became not only an exercise in creativity, but a history lesson! Eventually, Eric became interested in airplanes. For his high school graduation gift, he asked for flying lessons. Today, he's a licensed pilot and well on his way to a career in aviation.

Amy became interested in music and drama. She asked for piano lessons and became involved in our local community theater, where she's since starred in "Oliver!" and played minor roles in several other productions. At age sixteen, she is an accomplished pianist as well as a talented actress. She plans to pursue a career in film production and direction.

What more can I say? It was wonderful!

Q: Didn't they feel "out of it" when their friends talked about television programs?

A: If they did, they never complained about it (to us). I suspect it was somewhat frustrating for a while, but I'm sure they got lots of sympathy from their friends. In the final analysis, television gave them more time to socialize, and they not only developed more friends, but much better social skills. I'm sure the television industry would like us all to believe that children who don't watch television can't relate to their peers, but it simply isn't so. Over the years, I've talked to many other parents who've had the courage to remove television from their children's lives. They all say basically the same thing: The children become more imaginative, resourceful, self-sufficient, conversational, interesting, and outgoing. Never have I heard anything negative.

Q: When you reintroduced television into Eric and Amy's lives, how did you control it?

A: Four years after taking it away, we bought the smallest color portable then available and sat it on a bookshelf in the den. Every Sunday, the children went through the television listing and selected five hours worth of programs, at least two hours of which had to be educational. Using the following form, the children listed the programs they wanted to watch, along with days and times, and turned that list into us. If we approved, those became the shows—the only shows—they could watch. Substitutions were allowed, but had to be cleared in advance. In other words, if they missed one of the programs they had selected, they were not allowed to make up the time later in the week. This method works because it hands responsibility for enforcement over to the child or children. Because children would rather police themselves than be policed, they cooperate!

TELEVISION CONTRACT

CHILD'S NAME _____

FOR WEEK BEGINNING SUNDAY, _____

DAY	TIME	PROGRAM	LENGTH	APPROVED

Q: *If you had it to do over, what, if anything, would you and Willie do differently?*

A: We would not let the television-watching habit get started in the first place. An ounce of prevention is always better than a pound of cure.

READ
THIS
LAST!

So, there you have it. My six-point, guaranteed, call-me-a-bozo if you're not satisfied, plan for raising happy, healthy children. That's happy as in having good self-esteem, and healthy as in possessing a positive, achievement-oriented attitude toward the realities and challenges of life. To recap:

POINT ONE: Pay more attention to your marriage than you do to your children. In other words, put first things first and keep them there, where they're more likely to last. If you're a single parent, this translates: Pay slightly more attention to yourself than you do to your children. Remember, single parents, you can't successfully supply someone else's "warehouse" unless your own is fully stocked.

POINT TWO: Expect your children to obey. Stop apologizing for the decisions you make in their lives. Get back in touch with the power of "Because I said so." Stop thinking that you can persuade your children that your decisions are for their own good, or even that you need to try! Essential to a child's sense of security are parents who are authoritative, decisive, and trustworthy—in a word, powerful! So, get with it, folks! Your children are counting on you!

POINT THREE: Actualize your children's participation in the family by expecting and enabling them from an early age to make regular, tangible contributions to the family in the only form possible—chores. And along with making them responsible members of the family, make them responsible for their own behavior. Stop running after the bus, stop tying their shoes, stop trying to keep them from falling flat on their faces. Give them the opportunity to learn "the hard way," which is often the only way possible.

POINT FOUR: Give your children regular and realistic doses of Vitamin N. When you do, and they fall to the floor screaming, pat yourself on the back for a job well done. Remember that sufficient exposure to frustration not only prepares a child for the reality of adulthood, but gradually helps the child develop a tolerance for frustration. This tolerance results in perseverance, the key ingredient to every success story. Stop thinking that your first obligation is to make and keep them happy, because it isn't. Your first obligation is to endow them with the skills they will need to successfully pursue happiness on their own. Frustrate your children for success!

POINT FIVE: Where toys are concerned, less is more. And the more things any one toy can be, the better. Remember that when children tell us they're bored, they're really trying to tell us they've been given too much, too soon.

POINT SIX: Don't be misled by the accolades given certain children's programs. Remember that there's more going on than meets the eye when a child watches television, *any* television. Give your kids one of the most precious gifts of opportunity possible in this age of high-tech for the sake of high-tech: Growing years that aren't constantly sidetracked by the flicker of the plug-in drug. And finally . . .

POINT SEVEN: What's this?!! Point seven?!! But you said
. . . I know what I said. I said this was a Six-Point Plan.
Nevertheless, I can't leave without mentioning the seventh, and
perhaps the most important, point of all, which is: Love 'em
enough to do the first six!

ABOUT
THE
AUTHOR

John Rosemond is a family psychologist with Piedmont Psychological Associates of Gastonia, North Carolina. In his private practice, he specializes in working with parents, children, and families. John is also a member of the teaching faculty at the Pediatrics and Family Practice Departments of Charlotte Memorial Hospital.

Since 1978, John has written a nationally syndicated parenting column which currently appears in more than seventy-five newspapers across the United States and Canada. He is also the regularly featured parenting columnist for *Better Homes and Gardens* magazine.

His first book, *Parent Power! A Common-Sense Approach to Raising Your Children in the Eighties,* was published in 1981 by East Woods Press. *Parent Power!* was a Main Selection of the Young Parents Book Club and was released in paperback by Pocket Books in 1983.

In 1981, John was selected as "Professional of the Year" by the Mecklenburg County Mental Health Association of Charlotte, North Carolina. In 1986, he was presented with the Alumni Achievement Award by his alma mater, Western Illinois University.

Throughout the year, John is in considerable demand as a public speaker. His parenting presentations and workshops have drawn high marks from parent and professional groups all over the country.

Last, but by no means least, John is husband to Willie and father to Eric, twenty, and Amy, sixteen.

If you found this book useful, you'll be happy to know there are more from John Rosemond, America's most widely read parenting authority. Rosemond is the author of a series of parenting books from Andrews and McMeel. In addition to *John Rosemond's Six Point Plan for Raising Happy, Healthy Children,* two more books are available at your local bookseller:

Ending the Homework Hassle: Understanding, Preventing, and Solving School Performance Problems

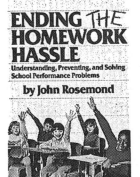

ENDING THE HOMEWORK HASSLE
Understanding, Preventing, and Solving School Performance Problems

by John Rosemond

Homework. It's one of the most time-consuming and frustrating of all childrearing issues. But it doesn't have to be.

In *Ending the Homework Hassle,* Rosemond guides parents through a practical, time-saving program that will put an end to their overinvolvement in what should be — needs to be — a child's primary responsibility.

But that's not all! Rosemond addresses just about every school performance problem imaginable. He discusses when and how to retain a child, when to seek remedial help (and how to choose the right help), how to motivate the underachiever, and what you should know about Attention Deficit Disorder — a syndrome that prevents tens of thousands of American children from doing their best in school.

Other books on homework encourage lots of parental involvement. Not this one. Rosemond's approach will help parents disengage from homework hassles as they manage their children toward even greater success in school.

Parent Power! A Common-Sense Approach to Parenting in the '90s and Beyond

Parent Power! is chock-full of practical, common sense solutions to problems encountered by parents of children of all ages.

Rosemond's approach in *Parent Power!* is developmental and problem-oriented. In it, he helps parents identify and understand the significance of each stage of a child's growth, anticipate the problems typical (and in some cases, not-so-typical) to each stage, and provides workable advice for resolving those problems.

Parent Power! was first published in 1981 by East Woods Press and was a Main Selection of the Young Parents Book Club in that year. It was later released in papcrback by Pocket Books. This new edition has been revised and updated to include chapters on teenagers, adoption, bedtimes battles, and divorce and custody. The developmental section has also been greatly expanded to cover a broader range of issues and topics.